Cambridge Elements ☰

Elements in Child Development
edited by
Marc H. Bornstein
National Institute of Child Health and Human Development, Bethesda
Institute for Fiscal Studies, London
UNICEF, New York City

GENDER IN CHILDHOOD

Christia Spears Brown
University of Kentucky

Sharla D. Biefeld
University of Kentucky

Michelle J. Tam
University of Kentucky

CAMBRIDGE
UNIVERSITY PRESS

CAMBRIDGE
UNIVERSITY PRESS

University Printing House, Cambridge CB2 8BS, United Kingdom

One Liberty Plaza, 20th Floor, New York, NY 10006, USA

477 Williamstown Road, Port Melbourne, VIC 3207, Australia

314–321, 3rd Floor, Plot 3, Splendor Forum, Jasola District Centre,
New Delhi – 110025, India

79 Anson Road, #06–04/06, Singapore 079906

Cambridge University Press is part of the University of Cambridge.

It furthers the University's mission by disseminating knowledge in the pursuit of
education, learning, and research at the highest international levels of excellence.

www.cambridge.org
Information on this title: www.cambridge.org/9781108812740
DOI: 10.1017/9781108874281

© Christia Spears Brown, Sharla D. Biefeld, and Michelle J. Tam 2020

First published 2020

A catalogue record for this publication is available from the British Library.

ISBN 978-1-108-81274-0 Paperback
ISSN 2632-9948 (online)
ISSN 2632-993X (print)

Cambridge University Press has no responsibility for the persistence or accuracy of
URLs for external or third-party internet websites referred to in this publication
and does not guarantee that any content on such websites is, or will remain,
accurate or appropriate.

Gender in Childhood

Elements in Child Development

DOI: 10.1017/9781108874281
First published online: October 2020

Christia Spears Brown
University of Kentucky

Sharla D. Biefeld
University of Kentucky

Michelle J. Tam
University of Kentucky

Author for correspondence: Christia Spears Brown, christia.brown@uky.edu

Abstract: Gender is a highly salient and important social group that shapes how children interact with others and how they are treated by others. In this Element, we offer an overview and review of the research on gender development in childhood from a developmental science perspective. We first define gender and the related concepts of sex and gender identity. Second, we discuss how variations in cultural context shape gender development around the world and how variations within gender groups add to the complexity of gender identity development. Third, we discuss major theoretical perspectives in developmental science for studying child gender. Fourth, we examine differences and similarities between girls and boys using the latest meta-analytic evidence. Fifth, we discuss the development of gender, gender identity, and gender socialization throughout infancy, early childhood, and middle childhood. We conclude with a discussion of future directions for the study of gender development in childhood.

Keywords: gender, stereotypes, development, gender socialization, gender identity

ISBNs: 9781108812740 (PB), 9781108874281 (OC)
ISSNs: 2632-9948 (online), ISSN 2632-993X (print)

Contents

1 Introduction

Walking through a toy store with aisles awash in pink or blue toys, watching a playground where the girls play in all-girl dyads and the boys play in all-boy groups, and listening to an elementary school teacher's greeting of "Good morning, girls and boys!" only begin to highlight how important gender is in children's lives. For most children, gender is arguably the single most salient and important social category in their lives. Gender is one of the first labels they learn about themselves. By the time they are in preschool, children have attitudes and stereotypes about how girls and boys should look, think, and behave. Gender shapes how parents, teachers, and peers interact with individual children. Yet much of the most meta-analytic research and research in neuroscience suggests that there are few actual differences between girls and boys. Furthermore, research shows that gender and gender identity are more complex and fluid than previously thought. Although researchers have examined gender development for more than sixty years – with one of the first books specifically about gender roles edited by Eleanor Maccoby in 1966 called *The Development of Sex Differences* (Maccoby, 1966) – research, with advances in neuroimaging, advanced statistical designs, and international samples, has revealed how complex gender development truly is.

In this Element, we offer an overview and review of the research on gender development in childhood from a developmental science perspective. We first define gender and contrast gender with the related concepts of sex and gender identity. Second, we discuss how variations in cultural context shape gender development around the world and how variations within gender groups add to the complexity of gender identity development. Third, we discuss major theoretical perspectives in developmental science for studying child gender. Fourth, we examine, using the latest meta-analytic evidence, differences and similarities between girls and boys in their emotions and aggression, play and toys, and cognitive skills. Fifth, we discuss the development of gender, gender identity, and gender socialization throughout infancy, early childhood, and middle childhood. We will focus on what children know and how children think about gender, how children learn about gender and gender stereotypes, and how gender impacts the emotional, social, and academic development of children. Last, we discuss future directions for the study of gender in childhood.

2 Defining Gender

Before describing the field of gender development, it is important to define what we mean when we say gender and how gender and sex overlap and how they are distinct. Throughout the developmental literature, gender and sex are often used interchangeably to refer to children's own gender identity, their sex assigned at birth, others' perceptions of children's gender identity, as well as behaviors and dress associated with gender (Muehlenhard & Peterson, 2011). Although these terms are sometimes used interchangeably, they are distinct constructs.

Biological *sex* refers to the categories of female and male determined by chromosomes, hormones, and genitalia. Specifically, depending on the chromosome contributed by the father, a developing fetus typically (but not always) has either two X chromosomes or an X and a Y chromosome. A gene on the short arm of the Y chromosome triggers the development of the testes, which in turn start secreting testosterone six weeks after conception. The testosterone (along with anti-Müllerian hormone) leads the fetus to develop as a male. If the Y chromosome is not present, it cannot override an important gene on the X chromosome (called DAX1) that signals the body to create ovaries. Without that override and the testes to produce testosterone, the fetus develops into a female, with ovaries that produce estrogen. These genetic and hormonal differences *in utero* lead to the development of sex-differentiated genitalia. Observation of external genitalia is how doctors typically identify the sex of the newborn infant, which is then recorded on the birth certificate. Although sex has traditionally been viewed as a binary (either female *or* male), this binary categorization is problematic and incomplete, as approximately 1 out of 100 infants are intersex, with some biological characteristics of males and some biological characteristics of females. Furthermore, there are a host of genetic and hormonal variations in which chromosomes do not always directly relate to hormones, genitalia, or secondary sex characteristics.

In contrast to sex, *gender* refers to the "meanings that societies and individuals ascribe to male and female categories" (Wood & Eagly, 2002, p. 699). An examination of gender development requires attention to the culturally ascribed meaning associated with gender and how individual children feel about that meaning. *Gender roles* are the behaviors, attitudes, and personality traits that are designated as either feminine or masculine in a given culture. Gender roles often reflect *gender stereotypes*, or the beliefs and expectations people hold about the typical characteristics, preferences, and behaviors of women/girls and men/boys. In terms of gender, "feminine" and "masculine" are recognized as independent and orthogonal continua, such that everyone has certain degrees of feminine and masculine traits and qualities. Gender is often marked by perceptually salient and differentiated sociocultural cues, such as differences in hair length, makeup, jewelry, or clothing. How individuals choose to communicate their gender to others through clothing, hairstyles, and mannerisms is referred to as their *gender expression.*

The concept of *gender identity* is more complex as it has been applied to slightly different concepts over time. Early research in gender development focused on how children learn their own gender and the gender labels of others, a concept referred to as gender identity (e.g., Slaby & Frey, 1975). For example, young children might be asked, when shown a girl doll or a boy doll, "Is this a girl or a boy?" They can also be asked, "Are you a girl or a boy?" This ability to identify one's own gender (i.e., having an "accurate" gender identity) was seen as the first step toward developing *gender constancy*, or the recognition that one's gender (as a function of one's sex) is a stable, unchanging characteristic of an individual (Kohlberg, 1966). Children first learn to identify their gender (e.g., "She is a girl" or "I am a boy"), followed by the more complicated tasks of recognizing that gender is stable across time (e.g., "I am a boy and will also be a boy when I grow up") and gender consistency across situations (e.g., "I am a boy and will still be a boy if I wear a dress"; Slaby & Frey, 1975).

More work has focused on the psychological meaning associated with gender, a concept also termed gender identity. Egan and Perry (2001) proposed a five-component model of gender identity, defined as individuals' feelings about their gender group, which consisted of (1) *membership knowledge* (i.e., knowledge of membership in a gender category); (2) *gender typicality* or compatibility (i.e., how typical individuals feel for their gender); (3) *felt pressure to conform* (i.e., how much individuals feel pressure to conform to traditional gender norms stemming from parents and peers); (4) *gender contentedness* (i.e., how happy or content individuals are to be their gender); and (5) *intergroup bias* (i.e., how much individuals believe that their gender is superior to the other gender). This model of gender identity has been highly influential in the field of gender development and helped highlight the ways in which children may feel *internal* contentment with their gender and *external* pressures to conform to gender norms. Martin and colleagues (2017) convincingly argued that the concept of gender compatibility needed to be expanded to recognize that an individual child could feel similar to their own gender but also (orthogonally) feel similar to the other gender. The distinction between own and other-gender similarity is important because, based on Egan and Perry's model of gender identity, it was unclear whether a child who felt low in gender typicality simply felt low in similarity to their own gender, felt a greater connection to the other gender (e.g., a girl who feels like a "tomboy"), or felt no connection to gender at all. Thus, Martin and colleagues (2017) revised the conception of gender identity to include an independent assessment of same-gender similarity as well as other-gender similarity.

Last, the term gender identity has been used to describe an individual's psychological sense of being female or male (or both or neither). If an individual's gender identity is consistent with their sex labeled at birth (usually based on external genitalia), they are referred to as *cisgender*; if their gender identity is not consistent with their sex labeled at birth, they are referred to as *transgender*. When equality and civil rights are discussed (e.g., when bills are passed, or not, to ban discrimination on the basis of gender identity), or when the acronym SOGIE (Sexual Orientation, Gender Identity, and Expression) is used, this form of gender identity is being referenced.

Some work has argued that sex and gender are so intertwined with one another and with cultural and social norms that it is difficult to parse them (for a review, see Hyde et al., 2019). Hyde and colleagues (2019) asserted that the term *gender/sex* is more appropriate to account for this complexity. For example, sex differences in neural development (typically seen as innate) may be influenced by differential media exposure based on gender (a social phenomenon). The term gender/sex also aids in challenging the traditional gender binary (Jordan-Young & Rumiati, 2012; van Anders, 2015). Current research in the fields of neuroscience and behavioral endocrinology has refuted the assertion of gender dimorphic brain and hormonal systems based on sex (Joel et al., 2015; van Anders, Goldey, & Bell, 2014). Additionally, psychological research has shown that children's tendency to view gender as a sex-based binary is not innate but instead a learned behavior that can be changed and possibly eliminated (Bigler & Liben, 2007).

3 The Variation of Gender across Individuals, Families, and Cultures

3.1 Diversity of Girls and Boys

Gender is a multidimensional construct that includes psychological, social, and behavioral components (WHO, 2018). As such, it is unsurprising that there is considerable individual diversity within gender categories. For example, there is variation in gender identity (Temkin et al., 2017), and gender identity may or may not fall within a female or male binary category. Unfortunately, even the term transgender assumes a gender binary (Ocha, 2012). Children who do not fit neatly within the binary distinctions of girl or boy may be described as non-binary, gender-nonconforming, gender-expansive, genderqueer, or gender-diverse. Evidence suggests that not conforming to rigid gender norms is relatively common. Research from the 1990s indicated that 39 percent of girls and 23 percent of boys exhibited ten or more behaviors that are considered non-conforming for their gender (Sandberg et al., 1993). A 2017 Harris Poll found that almost one in eight young people identify as gender-nonconforming or transgender.

Although research on gender development in transgender children has been rare, this area of work is rapidly expanding. Exact percentages are difficult to determine, but estimations suggest that, by middle school, approximately 1.3 percent of youth identify as transgender (Shields et al., 2013) and, by adulthood, approximately 2.4 percent of individuals identify as transgender (Tate, Ledbetter, & Youssef, 2013). In a 2016 survey completed by almost 81,000 adolescents in Minnesota, researchers asked, "Do you consider yourself transgender, genderqueer, genderfluid, or unsure about your gender identity?" They found that 3 percent of ninth and eleventh graders in Minnesota do not identify as a girl or boy, instead selecting one of the other, nonbinary options (Rider et al., 2018).

Particularly promising is research coming from the Trans Youth Project, which was launched in 2013 as a longitudinal research project examining gender development in socially transitioned, transgender children from three to twelve years old in North America (e.g., Fast & Olson, 2018; Olson et al., 2016; Olson & Gülgöz, 2018). This project is focused on a national, community-based sample contacted through support groups, conferences on gender identity, websites, and word of mouth. This sampling technique differs from much previous research, which primarily recruited samples through mental health clinics and thus confounded being transgender with having mental health concerns. This sample of prepubertal children both (1) explicitly identify as a different gender than labeled at birth (instead of merely "wishing" to be a different gender) and (2) have "socially transitioned," meaning they present themselves to others consistent with their gender identity rather than their sex labeled at birth. This transgender sample of children is compared to a matched sample of their gender-typical siblings (thus controlling for family characteristics) and to unrelated gender-matched children. Early findings indicate that transgender children (1) have similar gender development, (2) have similar gendered preferences (e.g., in toys and clothes), and (3) have fewer gender stereotypes than non-transgender (i.e., cisgender) children (Olson & Gülgöz, 2018). Although in its early stages, this work will help illuminate how gender development is both similar and unique across cisgender and transgender children.

There is also biological variability within cisgender girls and boys. For example, girls with congenital adrenal hyperplasia (CAH) are exposed to heightened levels of androgen *in utero*; thus, girls with CAH have hormone exposure more similar to males *in utero* than females. Studies of these children offer an important lens for investigating the role of gonadal hormones and socialization on behaviors and gender differences (Berenbaum & Hines, 1992). For example, research regarding early toy preferences found that girls with CAH preferred male stereotyped toys (such as cars and blocks) more than female stereotyped toys (such as dolls and kitchenware) and preferred male toys more than female controls who did not have CAH (Berenbaum & Hines, 1992). The difference in toy preference between girls with CAH and girls without CAH seems to be driven by the role of hormones, particularly androgens, in shaping early gender differences in play and toy preferences, more so than socialization. In their research, girls with CAH were socialized similarly to girls without CAH; indeed, parents of girls with CAH encouraged them to play with female-typical toys *more* than they encouraged girls without CAH. Yet their play more closely resembled that of boys than that of other girls (Pasterski et al., 2005). Thus, regardless of parental encouragement to play with girl-typical toys, girls with CAH still preferred male-typical toys. Furthermore, this difference does not seem to be unique to CAH per se, as boys with CAH did not differ from boys without CAH (Pasterski et al., 2005). This research illustrates how incorporating diverse samples offers important insights into mechanisms that may influence gender development.

3.2 Diversity of Family Gender Composition

In addition to individual diversity of gender for children, there is diversity of the gender composition of families. For example, parents may consist of mothers and fathers in the same household or in separate households (separated because of divorce, dissolution of the relationship, or because they never lived in the same household). After divorce, 81 percent of custodial parents are mothers and 18 percent are fathers (Cancian et al., 2014). Families also differ in the gender composition of the siblings in the families and the extent to which sisters and brothers are treated differently (McHale, Crouter, & Tucker, 1999). For example, they found that having both daughters and sons in the same family can actually exacerbate gender stereotypes by modeling and reinforcing gender-stereotypical behaviors and by serving as sources of social comparison. This happens when parents have both the opportunity to treat girls and boys differently and choose to do so because they endorse traditional gender roles.

Families may also consist of two mothers or two fathers. The number of households in which there is at least one sexual minority parent has been growing, and between 2 million and 3.7 million children under the age of eighteen in the United States have lesbian, gay, bisexual, and transgender parents (LGBT; Gates, 2015). However, based on cross-sectional and longitudinal studies with more than 100 families headed by either lesbian, gay, or heterosexual couples, children seem to develop in typical ways regardless of parental sexual orientation (Farr, 2016; Farr, Forssell, & Patterson, 2010). For example, in a study with eight-to-twelve-year-old children in the Netherlands from either lesbian-headed families or heterosexual families, researchers found that children in lesbian families showed less in-group bias favoring their own gender and felt less parental pressure to conform to gender stereotypes than children in heterosexual families (Bos & Sandfort, 2010). Children in lesbian families were also more open to and less certain about future heterosexual romantic relationships. There were no differences, however, in children's global self-worth and social competence. Similarly, longitudinal research with children with gay, lesbian, or heterosexual parents examined their gender-conforming and gender-nonconforming behaviors, assessed via parents' reports and observation of children's toy play, in preschool and then five years later (Farr et al., 2018). Researchers found that, although children's gender-typed behaviors varied across age and gender, there were no differences in gender conformity or nonconformity based on their parents' sexual orientation (Farr et al., 2018).

3.3 Diversity of Gender across Cultures

Most work focusing on gender development has been conducted in Western cultures. Yet, because gender is culturally constructed, it is important to look at gender across cultures.

At the country level, and across cultures within the same country, we see varying degrees of discrepancies between girls and boys (e.g., Bornstein et al., 2016). For example, in many parts of the world, parents exhibit strong preferences for sons over daughters (The Economist, 2010), often reflecting the sons' roles as future financial providers for the family. Relatedly, there are differences in the educational attainment of girls and boys across the world. In some low-income countries in which compulsory education is not required of all children, parents often send only their sons to school (UNESCO, 2010). The United Nations Educational, Scientific, and Cultural Organization (UNESCO) has focused much of their work on documenting gender parity for girls' and boys' education throughout the world. In their 2015 report, in which they documented girls' and boys' school lives, they note remarkable progress in gender equality between 2000 and 2015. For example, in 2000 only thirty-two countries reached gender parity in both primary and secondary education; by 2015 that number was sixty-two. In Southern Asia, in 1990, girls could be expected to receive only six years of education; they now receive about twelve years of education. Despite this progress, more than half of the countries who are included in the United Nations have not yet reached gender parity in primary and secondary education, and no countries in sub-Saharan Africa have. Girls remain out of school more than boys do, with 15 million girls worldwide never attending school at all (UNESCO, 2016). This lack of education leads to different developmental outcomes for girls and boys. Although gender gaps in literacy are shrinking, they are still apparent. In Bangladesh, for example, literacy is twice as high in boys than girls (48 percent versus 24 percent, respectively; see Stewart, Bond, Abdullah, & Ma, 2000). These gaps are reflected in adulthood as well, as women account for two-thirds of the 750 million adults worldwide without basic literacy skills. It is also important to recognize that gender gaps in educational attainment worldwide are more pronounced for ethnic minority girls, girls with disabilities, and girls from the poorest quintiles (UNESCO, 2016). For example, only 37.2 percent of the children with disabilities who attend school are female.

There are also cultural differences in expectations for girls and boys. For example, in Islamic cultures there is closer monitoring of girls than boys, and boys are given more unrestricted access to peers than girls (Stewart, Bond, Abdullah, & Ma, 2000). In low- and middle-income countries around the world, although there is variation between countries, boys are slightly more likely to be expected to work outside the home and girls are slightly more likely than boys to be assigned caregiving and excessive amounts of household chores (Bornstein et al., 2016). Girls and boys may also interpret these behaviors differently. In a study with Bangladeshi youth, girls who reported their parents' close supervision of them perceived their parents to be warmer, whereas boys who reported parents' close supervision perceived their parents as more dominating (Stewart, Bond, Abdullah, & Ma, 2000). These different perceptions have different implications for psychological outcomes. For example, in Pakistan, parental autonomy granting was important and positive for boys' outcomes but unrelated to girls' outcomes (Stewart, Bond, Ho et al., 2000). In other words, there is cultural diversity in how parents treat girls and boys and cultural diversity in the impact of that differential parenting on children.

On the other end of the spectrum, there are cultures with high levels of gender equality and egalitarianism. Sweden, for example, is ranked by the European Union (EU) as the most gender-equal society in the EU (European Union for Gender Equality, 2019). This distinction is reflected in their preschool practices. The Swedish government established a national curriculum for preschools specifically designed to counteract traditional gender stereotypes, gender roles, and gender patterns (Swedish National Agency for Education, 2011). Although not consistently implemented, the Swedish government has developed "gender-neutral" preschools called *Egalia*, the Swedish word for equality. In these preschools, teachers do not use gendered language (such as him and her), instead referring to individual children by their first names or as "hen," a gender-neutral pronoun. Shutts and colleagues (2017) found that young children who attended these gender-neutral schools, although they encoded others' gender to the same degree, were more interested in playing with unfamiliar other-gender children and scored lower on a gender-stereotyping measure compared to children in typical preschools.

Even within Western samples of families, culture, ethnicity, and social class moderate gender development. For example, previous research has shown that Latinx families are typically more traditional in socializing gender roles than European American families (Azmitia & Brown, 2002; Baca Zinn & Wells, 2000; Hondagneu-Sotelo, 1994; Valenzuela, 1999), with women being more likely to maintain relational ties with families and preserve the ethnic traditions and integrity of the culture than men (Gil & Vazquez, 1996; Phinney, 1990). As such, girls are often trained to carry on that tradition and are often expected to remain close to the home and family. Boys are expected to gain independence and autonomy (Raffaelli & Ontai, 2004; Suárez-Orozco & Qin, 2006) and thus are given more freedom, mobility, and privileges than are girls (Domenech Rodríguez, Donovick, & Crowley, 2009; Love & Buriel, 2007; Suárez-Orozco & Qin, 2006); girls, however, often have more restrictions and are more closely monitored than are their brothers (Raffaelli & Ontai, 2004; Suárez-Orozco & Qin, 2006). Furthermore, girls, on average, are assigned more chores and responsibilities than their brothers (Raffaelli & Ontai, 2004). One example is that Mexican American parents are more likely to choose their daughters than their sons to translate for them (i.e., language brokering); the increased demand for language brokering for daughters, however, typically involves tasks that can be completed within the home, such as filling out paperwork (Love & Buriel, 2007; Valenzuela, 1999). Not surprisingly, although both girls and boys respect and value their families (Valenzuela & Dornbusch, 1994), girls are socialized to be even more connected to their families than boys (Raffaelli & Ontai, 2004).

Beyond different expectations and experiences for girls and boys across countries and cultures, there are also cultural differences in the basic conceptions of gender and accepted gender identities. For thousands of years, a nonbinary category of individuals, called *hijras*, has been documented in India. In 2014, after years of extreme discrimination, the Supreme Court in India officially recognized *hijras*, as well as transgender people, as a "third gender." In Independent Samoa, some males identify as *fa'afafine*, which literally translated means "in the manner of a woman." They are males who are sexually attracted to men, often have a feminine gender expression, but do not identify as men or women (Vasey & Bartlett, 2007). Retrospective studies that compared the childhoods of *fa'afafine* individuals, men, and women found that *fa'afafine* individuals reported playing with girls' toys and games more often as children than did the women. They also reported believing they were girls as children and not feeling distressed by their identity (Condon & Stern, 1993).

3.4 Conclusion

Taken together, we see that discussions about gender cannot simply rely on discussion about differences between girls and boys. There is considerable diversity within gender groups, such that individual girls and individual boys differ from one another more than the average girl and average boy differ. There is variation among children with male genitalia and female genitalia, in that they may identify as either boys, girls, both, neither, or some gender-expansive or gender-creative combination. Our growing understanding of gender identity, still in its somewhat nascent stages, will continue to inform how gender and gender similarities and differences are determined. There is also considerable diversity in families regarding how gender is represented in both the parents and siblings. Finally, there is enormous diversity across cultures, both in terms of how girls and boys are treated and, at times, in how gender is even defined.

4 Theoretical Approaches to Gender Development

There are many different theoretical perspectives through which researchers have studied gender in childhood. Some theories focus on the ways in which gender is largely reflective of biological sex and focus their research questions on how biological markers such as secondary sex hormones and chromosomes might influence differential behaviors for females and males (e.g., Berenbaum & Hines, 1992). Many of these differences are attributed to differentiated neurological development that occurs *in utero*. Boys experience a four-month surge of testosterone ending in the second trimester that is critical to developing their genitalia. After birth, for about one to two months, boys get a second surge of testosterone and girls get a surge of estrogen (referred to as *mini-puberty*). Most biological differences in girls and boys are attributed to the differences that occur during these critical periods. Some evidence suggests, for example, that testosterone levels are related to play preferences (e.g., Berenbaum & Hines, 1992). Auyeung and colleagues (2009) found that *in utero* testosterone exposure was linked to gender differentiated play patterns, such that exposure to more testosterone was related to parent reports of more frequent male-typed play (such as rough-and-tumble play) for both girls and boys. Additionally, Kung and colleagues (2016) found that higher levels of testosterone during mini-puberty were related to a larger vocabulary size at eighteen to thirty months. Some researchers, however, have found no relation between testosterone exposure *in utero* and gender-typical play behavior or toy preference (Knickmeyer et al., 2005; van de Beek et al., 2009).

Other theoretical approaches have focused on the role of context, social environments, and cognition in shaping gender development. For example, social learning theory originally asserted that external environmental influences were the main drivers of gender development (Mischel, 1966). Social learning theory argues that gender roles are learned through reinforcement, punishment, and modeling, such that children are rewarded and reinforced for behaving in concordance with gender roles and punished for breaking gender roles. In addition, social learning theory argues that children learn many of their gender roles by modeling the behaviors of adults and older children and, in doing so, develop ideas about what behaviors are appropriate for each gender.

This emphasis on socialization is reflected in trends in gender research. In a 2011 analysis of gender development research in the journal *Sex Roles*, Zosuls and colleagues (2011) documented that most research on gender development in the 1960s and 1970s (at least, the research published in *Sex Roles*) concentrated on parents' socialization of girls and boys through different expectations and attitudes toward their children. This approach was ultimately limited, however, because parent socialization practices could not fully explain the high degree of gender-stereotypical behaviors among children (Lytton & Romney, 1991).

Newer theories incorporated children's own cognitive processes into learning from the environment. Social cognitive theory (Bussey & Bandura, 1999), for example, incorporates cognitive perspectives into social learning and asserts that children's conceptions of gender roles are the result of a broad network of social influences, which operate interdependently from one another in different contexts. The focus is on how children contribute to their own gender development through "agentic actions within the interrelated systems of influence" (Bussey & Bandura, 1999, p. 1). One way children seek out same-gender-consistent information, according to social cognitive theory, is by modeling relevant others (Bussey & Bandura, 1999). When children attend to same-gender models (i.e., girls to mothers and boys to fathers), and those models engage in gender-stereotype-consistent behaviors, children's own behaviors and attitudes become stereotype-consistent.

Similarly, gender schema theory (Bem, 1981) asserts that children are active contributors to their gender development in that they organize people's actions into categories or schemas, such as "girls" and "boys." As children observe the world, gender categories become associated with activities and behaviors (e.g., girls cooking and boys playing with trucks). Gender schema theory argues that children are motivated to be prototypical members of their gender group, as being prototypical helps with both self-definition and cognitive consistency

(Martin & Ruble, 2010). Children recognize their own gender category within the first two years of life. Afterwards, they seek out same-gender-consistent information, ignore information relevant for the other gender, and misremember gender-inconsistent information (Martin & Halverson, 1983; Martin, Ruble, & Szkrybalo, 2002). For example, in experimental studies, when children were shown a picture of a girl sawing wood, they later misremembered the picture as a boy sawing wood (Martin & Halverson, 1983). In this way, by only correctly remembering schema-consistent information and altering disconfirming information to fit their existing stereotypes, gender schemas strengthen over time. Further, children seek out experiences that fit their existing gender schema. For example, when children were given a novel toy and told that it was a toy that one gender typically likes, children of that gender preferred the toy over a toy described as being for the other gender (Martin, Eisenbud, & Rose, 1995). Thus, children are self-socializing and actively constructing their own gender development based on their own cognitions about what is appropriate for their gender. Recent research suggests that this process of self-socializing in accordance with one's gender identity is similar for both cisgender and transgender children, as transgender children, like cisgender children, also seek out information consistent with their internal gender identity (Gülgöz et al., 2019).

Consistent with the basic concept that children actively construct their own gender development, developmental intergroup theory (DIT) asserts that gender is an important category to young children because culture treats it as such, which leads children to begin to sort their world into gendered categories (Bigler & Liben, 2007). Specifically, DIT postulates that children are attuned to the social groups that are treated as important within a given culture. For example, adults' heavy focus on gender, such as verbally labeling individual children ("What a smart girl!") and groups of children ("Good morning, girls and boys!") and color-coding toys and clothes into pink and blue, enhances both the perceptual and the psychological salience of gender categories. The repeated use of a gender as a functional group leads children to pay attention to gender as a key source of information about themselves and others. Children, in turn, seek out and encode any possible gender differences and form rigid stereotypes based on gender. Those stereotypes are subsequently difficult to change (because, as described, children have better memory for information that confirms their stereotypes). This theory has been empirically supported in experimental classrooms in which teachers were asked to use gender in a functional way, such as to sort and organize children into groups ("Line up boy, girl, boy, girl"), to segregate their seating ("Boys sit on the left, girls on the right"), and to provide two distinct bulletin boards, one pink and one blue (Bigler, 1995). Relative to children in classrooms that ignored gender as a functional category, children in the gendered classroom developed stronger gender stereotypes after six weeks. Similar studies have replicated this effect when teachers made comparable functional use of novel groups based on whether students were assigned a red or blue tee shirt (Bigler, Brown, & Markell, 2001; Brown & Bigler, 2002). When teachers ignored the color groups, children did not develop stereotypes based on the groups; however, when teachers treated the groups as meaningful, children developed biases on the basis of those groups. Thus, DIT combines social and cognitive theories to describe why gender stereotypes are so easily constructed and maintained.

5 Gender Differences and Similarities in Childhood

A large portion of the literature on gender development has focused on examining gender differences across childhood and psychological domains. Because of the massive amounts of published studies exploring gender differences, there are also a large number of published meta-analyses across various psychological domains. Some meta-analyses have confirmed that, although gender differences exist, they are often small; they have also shown that the size and direction of effects can vary at different points of development and in different contexts (Hyde, 2005; Hyde, Fennema, & Lamon, 1990). Although gender differences have been investigated in many different domains, we focus on three of the most common childhood differences explored: (1) emotions and aggression, (2) play and toys, and (3) cognitive skills. We also discuss the importance of recognizing gender similarities.

5.1 Emotions and Aggression

One of the most commonly examined gender differences is focused on differing emotional expressions and behaviors between girls and boys. Gender differences in temperament and emotionality have been investigated in infants as young as two months old (Bornstein et al., 2015). Research regarding the stability of temperament has shown few differences between girls and boys (e.g., Bornstein et al., 2015); however, there are exceptions. In one study of seventy-three infants, girls showed slightly more stable positive affectivity (e.g., smiling, laughing, and being soothed) than boys, from two to thirteen months old (Bornstein et al., 2015). Evidence also suggests that gender differences in temperament appear to be very small in infancy but increase slightly by school age (Else-Quest et al., 2006). For example, one meta-analysis of 189 studies investigated temperament in children from 3 months to 13 years old. Results revealed that gender differences were either statistically small or nonexistent in most dimensions of emotion and that there were no gender differences in general emotionality, shyness, sadness, or anger (Else-Quest et al., 2006). There were, however, differences across some dimensions. Most notably, there was a relatively large gender difference in effortful control, as girls demonstrated better effortful control than boys, were better at managing and regulating their attention, and were moderately better at inhibiting their impulses (Else-Quest et al., 2006). Boys were also slightly less able to suppress inappropriate responses and slightly more likely to blurt things out than girls were (Else-Quest et al., 2006). There was also a small but significant gender difference in high-intensity pleasure and in overall activity levels, such that boys demonstrated more pleasure from high-intensity activities and had overall higher activity levels than girls (Else-Quest et al., 2006).

An additional meta-analysis focused on gender differences in the facial, vocal, and behavioral expressions of different types of emotions in children and also found few gender differences (Chaplin & Aldao, 2013). In this study, which analyzed 555 effect sizes from 166 studies, the authors reported very small gender differences in both positive and internalizing emotions (e.g., sadness, anxiety, sympathy), with girls showing slightly more frequent emotion expression than boys. The authors identified important moderators, however, that contextualized those small differences. For example, the gender differences in positive emotions expanded as children got older, with the difference almost nonexistent in early childhood but more pronounced in adolescence. Although boys showed more externalizing emotions than girls in toddlerhood and middle childhood, they showed fewer externalizing emotions than girls in adolescence (Chaplin & Aldao, 2013). In other words, assumptions about gender differences in emotion are really dependent on the age group in question (among other factors).

Another area of emotional development and behavior that is frequently examined for gender differences is aggression. Indeed, aggression is one of the most frequently examined gender differences in childhood, as is evidenced by multiple published meta-analyses (Archer, 2004; Knight et al., 2002; Loeber, Capaldi, & Costello, 2013). Overall, evidence suggests that boys exhibit higher rates of aggression than girls in some, but not all, contexts (Archer, Pearson, & Westeman, 1988; Crick & Grotpeter, 1995; Hyde, 1984). For example, one meta-analysis of gender differences in aggression investigated 273 studies with 197 effect sizes and found that 88.8 percent of the effect sizes indicated that boys were more aggressive than girls; however, 10.6 percent of the effect sizes illustrated the opposite effect, that girls were more aggressive than boys (Knight et al., 2002). In a review of forty-six different meta-analysis, Hyde (2005) concluded that boys have reliably higher rates of physical aggression than girls. Other forms of aggression, however, are less reliably different; for example, for relational aggression, girls appear more relationally aggressive when measured with direct observation, less so when measured with peer or teacher ratings, and not at all when measured with self-reports (Archer, 2004; Crick & Grotpeter, 1995; Hyde, 2005; Knight et al. 2002). Meta-analysis also indicate that emotional arousal impacts gender differences in aggression, such that gender differences are larger in studies that produced small to medium increases in emotional arousal and smallest when there was either no emotional arousal or a lot of emotional arousal (Knight et al., 2002). Overall, research on gender differences in aggression illustrates that many factors, including the type of aggression, how aggression is measured, and emotional arousal in response to aggression, impact the direction and magnitude of gender differences.

Researchers have also investigated at which point in development gender differences in aggression are most pronounced. Evidence suggests that gender differences are largest early in life (under six years of age) and decline with age (Hyde, 1984). When these gender differences in aggression first appear, however, is not clear. One study of children under the age of two in Quebec, Canada, found that gender differences in physical aggression were apparent at seventeen months, such that young boys were more physically aggressive than girls (Baillargeon et al., 2007). However, studies of children in the Netherlands and the United Kingdom found no gender differences in aggression until children entered toddlerhood (Alink et al., 2006; Hay, 2017; Hay et al., 2011). In these studies, gender differences in physical aggression began to emerge at about twenty-four months (Alink et al., 2006; Hay et al., 2011).

Given these complex differences, there is likely an intricate interplay between biological and socialization influences that affect the ways in which girls and boys express aggression. Indeed, the reasons for gender differences in aggression are highly contested, as some argue that sexual selection has led boys and men to be more aggressive (see Archer, 2009), some argue that the differences are hormonal and dictated by testosterone (see Book, Starzyk, & Quinsey, 2001), and others argue that socialization impacts this behavior more so than biology (see Wood & Eagly, 2002). Some research suggests that broader cultural gender differences are important. For example, Swiss researchers compared aggression in a large sample of immigrant children, living in Switzerland, whose parents migrated from countries that varied in gender equality (Nivette et al., 2014). They found that boys, especially in middle childhood, showed more physically aggressive behaviors than girls, and girls showed more prosocial behavior than boys. Critically, they also found that boys whose families came from countries with high levels of gender inequality were more likely to be aggressive than boys whose families came from countries with low levels of gender inequality. Furthermore, the gender differences between girls and boys were more exaggerated in children whose families came from countries with high levels of gender inequality. Consistent with cross-cultural findings, research has shown that fathers who held stronger gender stereotypes used more physical control with boys than with girls, and this differential treatment was related to larger gender differences in aggression (Endendijk et al., 2017). The inverse was found for fathers with counter-stereotypical beliefs, such that they used more physical control with girls, which in turn predicted girls' levels of aggression.

Taken together, research on gender differences in emotional expression and aggression suggests that there are gender differences in effortful control and physical aggression but that those differences are moderated by the particular period of development being studied, the ways in which the domain is conceptualized and measured, and contextual and socialization differences.

5.2 Play and Toys

Some of the biggest gender differences in childhood are seen in the play styles and toy preferences of children (for a review, see Weisgram & Dinella, 2018). Beginning in preschool and increasing throughout middle childhood, children tend to play in highly gender-segregated groups, such that girls play with girls and boys play with boys (Fabes, Martin, & Hanish, 2003; Maccoby, 1998; Maccoby & Jacklin, 1987; Ruble & Martin, 1998). Although about 10 to 24 percent of children's play interactions occur in mixed-gender groups, girls are more likely to play in mixed-gender groups than are boys (Bohn-Gettler et al., 2010; Fabes et al., 2003; Maccoby, 1998; Martin & Fabes, 2001). There are also differences in the types of play and activities children engage in. Most notably, boys typically play in organized rough-and-tumble games in large groups and are more likely to play away from adults; in contrast, girls often engage in less physically active play, play in smaller groups, and play in closer proximity to adults relative to boys (Fabes et al., 2003; Maccoby, 1998). Girls who have high activity play seem to face some social rejection from their peers, whereas boys who engage in high activity play do not (Bohn-Gettler et al., 2010). Although gender segregation can be partially attributed to differences in play styles, the link between similar play and same-gender peer groups was only found for boys and not for girls (Martin et al., 2011). Ironically, beyond differences in actual play styles, children's choices to segregate are also a function of children's *beliefs* that girls are more similar to girls than they are to boys and vice versa (Martin et al., 2002; Martin et al., 2011).

One of the largest gender differences in children's play is in their toy preferences (Weisgram & Dinella, 2018). Toys that are conceptualized as girls' toys tend to be associated with nurturing or household activities (such as caring for babies), and toys conceptualized as boys' toys tend to be associated with danger and propulsion (such as toy guns and trucks; Blakemore & Center, 2005). Research has consistently shown that girls, on average, show preferences for female stereotyped toys, such as dolls, and boys prefer masculine stereotyped toys, such as trucks (Ruble, Martin, & Berenbaum, 2006). Gender differences in toy preferences are shown as early as six months, with boys looking longer at trucks than dolls; however, both girls and boys prefer dolls over trucks at this age (Alexander, Wilcox, & Woods, 2009). These gender differences increase after age three as children enter early and middle childhood (Ruble et al., 2006).

Explanations for gender differences in toy preferences differ. Some researchers suggest that boys prefer toys that have propulsion properties because of biological preference for propulsive movement (Benenson, Tennyson, & Wrangham, 2011). One study directly tested this hypothesis by creating novel propulsion toys and examining whether preschool children preferred feminine, masculine, or gender-neutral propulsive toys (Dinella, Weisgram, & Fulcher, 2017). They found that, overall, children preferred gender-neutral toys, and they found no gender difference in preference for propulsion toys; however, girls were more flexible in their toy preferences and played with masculine, feminine, and gender-neutral toys more than boys (Dinella et al., 2017).

There is also substantial evidence that children's preferences for gender-stereotyped toys is largely driven by their knowledge of which toys are designated for girls and which for boys, and not the toys per se (see Dinella & Weisgram, 2018). The role of gender stereotypes in toy preference is exacerbated by toy companies focusing on gender stereotypes in both the design and the marketing of toys. For example, when novel toys were described with gender labels (e.g., "for boys"), the labels drove children's play behavior (and memory for the toys) more than the toy itself (e.g., Martin et al., 1995). Further, girls spend longer playing with toys labeled for girls and color-coded pink, whereas boys spend longer playing with toys labeled for boys and color-coded blue; this pattern holds regardless of the type of toy. In this way, toy play becomes a critical way that children reinforce their own stereotypes. This tendency to play with gender-coded toys has been documented across North America and China (e.g., Yeung & Wong, 2018). Fulcher and Hayes (2017) even found that the gender-typed color of the toys changed children's performance with the toy. Children, for example, took longer to build feminine objects with blue LEGO bricks than with pink bricks (Fulcher & Hayes, 2017).

Overall, research on gender differences in play styles and toy preferences indicates that girls have more flexibility in their play than boys, whereas boys engage in more stereotypical play (Dinella et al., 2017; Fabes et al., 2003; Martin & Fabes, 2001). Although biological differences in activity level may lead to more rough-and-tumble play among boys early on, many of the gender differences seen in toy preferences are likely influenced by the high degree of gendered marketing of toys as girl toys or boy toys.

5.3 Academic Skills and Attitudes

Research on gender differences in academic skills has focused primarily on language and math competencies. In terms of language development, on average, girls develop and acquire language more quickly than boys (Bornstein, Hahn, & Haynes, 2004; Hyde, 2005; Skeat et al., 2010; Zambrana, Ystrom, & Pons, 2012). Girls have also been shown to have larger vocabularies than boys, learn sentence structure faster than boys, and score higher on language development tests than boys (Bornstein et al., 2004; Hyde, 2005; Merz et al., 2015; Skeat et al., 2010; Zambrana et al., 2012). Additionally, boys are more likely to be placed in speech therapy and to be diagnosed with a speech impediment (Department of Health, 2004; Hammer, Farkas, & Maczuga, 2010; Whitehouse, 2010).

Not only are there gender differences in language and grammar acquisition but there are also differences in how girls and boys use language. For example, one meta-analysis of gender differences in language use across seventy-three independent samples of children (ranging from one year to seventeen years old) found that girls are more likely than boys to offer praise, to agree with the person they are talking to, and to elaborate on the other person's comments; boys, in contrast, are more likely than girls to assert their opinion and offer criticisms (Leaper & Smith, 2004). Although this language difference decreases in adolescence, these trends do continue into adulthood, depending on context (Leaper & Ayres, 2007).

Substantial research has also examined gender differences in mathematical competencies, abilities, and attitudes. Early math skills begin to develop when children are infants, as children first develop the concept of numeracy (recognizing that one item is less than two items). Kersey and colleagues analyzed gender differences in mathematical cognition, drawing data from five published studies with unpublished data from longitudinal records, to include more than 500 children ranging in age from 6 months to 8 years (Kersey et al., 2018). They focused on three key milestones of numerical development: numerosity perception, culturally trained counting, and formal and informal elementary mathematics concepts. They found no gender differences in six-month-old infants' ability to recognize numeracy change. Additionally, they found no gender differences in early formal math skills (such as numeral names), informal math skills (such as reasoning about quantitative relations), numerosity perceptions, or counting ability.

Differences in math abilities across girls and boys have changed over historical eras. In 1990, a meta-analysis indicated that girls were better at simple computation in elementary and middle school, whereas boys were better at complex problem-solving in high school (Hyde et al., 1990). Almost twenty years later, however, a new meta-analysis, as well as an analysis of statewide math standardized tests, indicated that there were no longer gender differences in any domains of mathematics performance (Hyde et al., 2008; Lindberg et al., 2010).

Although math skills and performance do not differ by gender, there are remaining gender differences in children's *beliefs* about their math ability and skills. For example, in international samples, boys have more confidence and less anxiety in math than girls (e.g., Hyde, 2005). Worldwide, girls on average have lower self-efficacy ratings, greater anxiety, and less confidence in STEM (science, technology, engineering, and math) subjects than boys have, despite outperforming boys across those school subjects. Even in the most gender-equal countries in the world, and despite the evidence of their own grades, girls and boys still show consistent gaps in confidence in STEM abilities (OECD, 2015). There are also gender differences in how children spend their out-of-school time that may be related to their later confidence in STEM subjects (OECD, 2015). Specifically, one-third of students across the forty-two countries that are part of the Organisation for Economic Co-operation and Development (OEDC) have used a computer before they start school at the age of six. Among those students, boys are 8 percentage points more likely than girls to have used a computer before the age of six. Thus, gender differences in STEM, particularly in domains such as computer science, may not be surprising if boys are more likely to have early experiences with computers.

5.4 Gender Similarities

Thus far we have reviewed gender differences in multiple domains and across children's development. However, Hyde has argued that the gender similarities hypothesis, which asserts that girls and boys are more similar than they are different, is a better way to conceptualize how girls and boys develop (Hyde, 2005; Hyde et al., 2019). This idea is not new; in 1974, Maccoby and Jacklin assessed more than 2,000 studies on gender differences and concluded that gender differences were absent in most psychological domains (Maccoby & Jacklin, 1974) . Despite early work acknowledging that gender similarities are more common than are differences, more attention has been given to gender differences. To test the magnitude and commonality of gender differences, Hyde (2005) proposed and tested the gender similarities hypothesis through a review of forty-six different meta-analyses. She found that, across domains of cognitive abilities, communication, personality and social variables, psychological well-being, and motor behaviors, gender differences were usually either very small or nonexistent. Indeed, 78 percent of all the effect sizes examined indicated no or very small differences. The only exceptions to the gender similarity hypothesis related to motor performance (such as throwing distance and velocity), some measures of sexuality (such as frequency of masturbation), and physical aggression (Hyde, 2005).

Research in neuroscience has provided some explanations for why girls and boys are more similar than different across most domains of development. Most notably, in a large-scale analysis of magnetic resonance imaging (MRI) of more than 1,400 brains (from 4 datasets), results indicated that there is considerable overlap between female and male brains. Researchers examined gender differences across all regions of the brain, as well as regions that are known to show the largest gender differences. They looked at differences in gray and white matter, structure, size, and connectivity. Across all areas they found that women's and men's brains are not sexually dimorphic (either female or male); instead, women's and men's brain structures are actually more similar to each other than they are different. There was extensive overlap between all gray matter, white matter, and neural connections (Joel et al., 2015). They also found that there was no such thing as a binary, prototypical female or prototypical male brain. Instead, Joel and colleagues (2015, p. 15472) found that "each brain is a unique mosaic of features, some of which may be more common in females compared with males, others may be more common in males compared with females, and still others may be common in both females and males." They corroborated those findings with a study of the personality, traits, attitudes, interests, and behaviors of more than 5,500 individuals, again finding a mosaic, rather than a dichotomy, of traits. In other words, instead of having a "pink brain" or "blue brain," most people have brains that are partially pink, partially blue, and partially a hybrid of the two. Taken together, large meta-analyses in psychological and academic domains, along with neurological research, lend support to the gender similarities hypothesis that girls and boys are actually more similar than they are different.

6 Gender and Gender Socialization across Development

Children begin to learn about gender almost from the moment they are born. Beginning in infancy, children learn about gender as a category, learn about their own gender, and learn stereotypes associated with gender. Gender-related knowledge, beliefs, and attitudes continue to develop through childhood. In the following sections, we highlight some of the key milestones in the development of gender and children's understanding of gender from infancy to twelve years old. For each developmental period, we also discuss how children learn about gender via contextual and social influences, such as parents, peers, teachers, and media.

6.1 Gender in Infancy

Infancy (defined here as birth until two years of age) is a critical period of enormous cognitive, social, emotional, and physical development (Bornstein, Arterberry, & Lamb, 2013). Infancy also represents a time in which children rapidly learn to process complex social information. Given how much focus cultures place on gender from birth (from the first time someone asks a pregnant woman "Do you know what you are having?" to the moment the doctor announces, "It is a girl!" or "It is a boy!"), it is not surprising that attention to and knowledge of gender begins very early in children's life.

6.1.1 Gender Development

Although most research has focused on how infants categorize the binary categories of women and men, evidence does show that infants can categorize individuals by gender very early in life (e.g., Ramsey-Rennels & Langlois, 2006). In infancy, categorical knowledge is often indicated by measuring an infant's differential responses to stimuli that belong to different categories. Investigating categorization abilities can include measuring how long an infant looks at a female face versus a male face (assessing whether they show a preference for one face over the other) or can involve showing repeated faces of one category (such as a series of female faces) until the infant gets bored (referred to as habituation) and assessing whether the infant shows renewed interest when presented with a face from a new category (such as a male face).

Some research suggests that, by three to four months, infants can distinguish between women's and men's faces by showing preference for faces that are the same gender as their primary caregiver; for example, infants with male primary caregivers prefer male faces, and infants with female primary caregivers prefer female faces (Quinn et al., 2002). At around six months old, infants can distinguish between female and male voices (Miller, 1983). Shortly after, at about nine months, infants are able to visually distinguish between women's and men's faces, regardless of the gender of their primary caregivers (Leinbach & Fagort, 1993). At about the same age, infants can reliably match a female face to a female voice (Poulin-Dubois et al., 1994) but cannot do the same for male faces and voices until about eighteen months. Across infancy, infants seem to be better at processing female faces and voices than male faces and voices (Poulin-Dubois, Serbin, & Derbyshire, 1998; Ramsey-Rennels & Langlois, 2006). This difference is likely due to both greater exposure and experiences with female faces (as women are more frequently the primary caregiver than men), as well as the greater perceptual variability of male faces compared to female faces (Ramsey, Langlois, & Marti, 2005).

About midway through the second year, infants begin to understand basic cultural gender associations and stereotypes. For example, at around eighteen months old, infants can associate female and male faces with "metaphorical" gender-stereotypical objects, such as associating a hammer, fire hat, fir tree, and bear with a male face (Eichstedt et al., 2002; see also Levy & Haaf, 1994). Girls (but not boys) are also able to associate gender-stereotypical toys with girls' and boys' faces (e.g., a doll to a girl face and a truck to a boy face). Between eighteen and thirty months, children also can correctly identify their own gender, can match a gender label (e.g., lady, man, girl, boy) with a female or male face, and can correctly sort pictures into piles of females and males (Levy, 1999; Martin & Ruble, 2010; Poulin-Dubois et al., 1998; Stennes, 2005). Around this age, infants also begin showing preferences for gender-stereotypical toys that match their own gender (Serbin et al., 2001).

After developing the ability to correctly categorize and identify gender, and coinciding with spurts in language development, children begin to verbally use gender labels. In a diary study, Zosuls and colleagues (2009) collected biweekly language inventories from mothers of children ranging from ten to twenty-one months. The researchers were interested in children's spontaneously used words rather than the verbal labels they used in artificial laboratory-based procedures. By around nineteen months, children spontaneously used gender labels, such as girl, boy, man, woman, lady, or guy, across contexts and individual referents. Additionally, children used gender labels for children referents (e.g., girl and boy) more than adult referents. After children acquired gender labels, their motivation to play in gender-typical ways increased (i.e., self-socialization). For example, when researchers provided children with gender-stereotypical toys (e.g., a truck and baby doll), moderately gender-stereotypical toys (e.g., wooden blocks and a tea set), and gender-neutral toys (e.g., a telephone and nesting cups), they found that young children who used more spontaneous gender labels were, in turn, more likely to play with the gender-stereotypical toys.

Some evidence also suggests that girls may develop gender-based knowledge earlier, and perhaps have more well-developed gender schemas, than boys. For example, girls can match female and male faces to voices earlier and more accurately than boys (Poulin-Dubois et al., 1998). Girls, on average, produce gender labels a month earlier ($M = 18.12$ months) than boys ($M = 19.39$ months) and are more likely to have produced gender labels between 17 and 21 months than boys (Zosuls et al., 2009). Similarly, around 18 months old, girls, but not boys, associate gender-stereotypical toys with the corresponding gender (Serbin et al., 2001).

6.1.2 Socialization in Infancy

Because gender is, by definition, socially defined and constructed, it is important to examine the social sources of influence that may contribute to children's gender development. Primary caregivers, such as parents, are important influences on infants' gender development and begin to emphasize gender before a child is even born.

In 2008, the first "gender reveal" party, a party hosted by expectant parents for their friends and family to publicly reveal the sex of their expected child, was posted online. In the decade that followed, more than 29,800,000 gender reveal videos were posted on YouTube and more than 62,700,000 gender reveal posts were made on Instagram (Giesler, 2019). These gender reveal parties can range from expectant parents cutting a cake to reveal pink or blue batter, to opening a box to reveal pink or blue balloons that float into the air, to skydiving with a pink or blue parachute. Not only are these gender reveal parties increasingly elaborate and expensive, but there are also reported instances in which they have been dangerous. One common method for the gender reveal is releasing colored powder into the air. In October 2019, a woman was killed at a US gender reveal party in Iowa when the homemade pipe bomb meant to explode and shoot pink or blue powder into the air misfired and hit her with flying debris (Garcia, 2019). In 2018, a US Border Patrol agent in Arizona held a gender reveal party that sparked a fire causing more than \$8 million in damage and burning more than 45,000 acres of land. Importantly, the name of the parties is misleading, as they are actually revealing the external genitalia of the baby (as identified by the doctor based on a sonogram image) and not the *gender*. Knowledge of the baby's presumed gender is further indicated by parents' choices of gendered first names, pink or blue bedroom decorations, and gender-specific clothing and haircuts (Leaper, 2015; MacPhee & Prendergast, 2019 Pomerleau et al., 1990). Additionally, the focus on gendered home environments and bedrooms has changed little since the 1970s. Rheingold and Cook (1975) originally found that young children's rooms and toys were highly gendered and MacPhee and Prendergast (2019) found similar results for children's bedrooms in 2017.

Beyond an overall focus on gender distinctions at birth, parents also emphasize gender by interacting differently with daughters versus sons. One common way that parents differentiate between girls and boys is through their language. Some research suggests that parents are more talkative with their daughters than with their sons (Brachfeld-Child, Simpson, & Izenson, 1988; Leaper, Anderson, & Sanders, 1998; Vandermaas-Peeler et al., 2012), a trend that may be especially prominent with newborns and that may decrease over time (Johnson et al., 2014; see also Gilkerson, Richards, & Topping, 2017). For example, in studies of parent–child interactions while reading books, mothers talked more with newborn daughters than sons (Johnson et al., 2014; see also Gilkerson et al., 2017). Parents have also been shown to use verbal direction more with girls than boys. In one study, while instructing their eight-month-old infants to put a cube into a cup, parents used more imperatives (e.g., instruction), negatives (e.g., preventing an action), and exhortations (e.g., "come on") with daughters than sons (Brachfeld-Child et al., 1988).

Research using new technologies suggests that the gender differences in how parents and children interact may really be driven by the gender of the parent, at least early on in development. Bergelson and colleagues (2019), using "wearable technology," had children in their first two years of life wear an audio recorder in the chest pocket of a special shirt. They then selected one day's worth of recording from each of the sixty-one children in their sample and catalogued each day-long recording into distinct audio clips, examining the quantity and proportion of child-directed and adult-directed speech that children heard over their first two years. Although they found no differences between how much speech girls and boys heard, they found that children heard two to three times more speech from females than males (Bergelson et al., 2019).

In addition to interacting differently with girls and boys, parents may also have different expectations for their daughters versus their sons. For example, one study of mothers and their eleven-month-old infants found that, although there was no actual gender difference in infants' crawling abilities, mothers of boys accurately estimated their child's crawling ability, whereas mothers of girls underestimated their child's crawling ability (Mondschein, Adolph, & Tamis-LeMonda, 2000). Furthermore, mothers of boys overestimated the steepest slope their child would attempt to crawl down, but mothers of girls underestimated the steepest slope their child would attempt to crawl down (Mondschein et al., 2000). Thus, although not based on actual observed differences, parents often hold gendered expectations for girls and boys. These expectations have the potential to shape children's future development and may explain some gender differences later in childhood (Blakemore, Berenbaum, & Liben, 2013).

6.2 Gender in Early Childhood

In early childhood (the years capturing toddlerhood and preschool), children are developing greater social cognition (e.g., theory of mind), develop stronger preferences and intentions (succinctly articulated by the label "terrible twos"), begin to develop a basic sense of self that is distinct from others, begin interacting with peers at school, and begin to consume children's media. These changes contribute to the growing complexity and stability of children's knowledge of gender and their own gender identity.

6.2.1 Gender Development

Early childhood, beginning around age three, marks a substantial increase in children's attention to, stereotypes associated with, and identification with gender. Some theorists have argued that this is the age when children first start to be influenced by cultural norms and start to become group-minded (Tomasello, 2019). Indeed, this is the age when many parents start to notice that their previously gender-neutral children start to show strong preferences aligned with their identified gender.

Most children consistently identify their own gender identity as early as two years old (Leinbach & Fagot, 1986; Zosuls et al., 2009). Children typically perceive themselves to be more similar to their own gender than the other gender (Martin et al., 2017). This is true of children who identify with their gender assigned at birth as well as transgender children who identify with a different gender than the one assigned at birth (Olson & Gülgöz, 2018). Beginning around age two or three, children also endorse gender stereotypes about roles, toys, and activities (see Ruble & Martin, 1998; for a review, see Zosuls et al., 2009). For example, classic research found that children, by age three, stereotyped girls as the ones "who cry," "like to play with dolls," "like to help their mother," and "like to cook"; boys are stereotyped as "like to play with cars," "like to build things," "like to help their father," and "say 'I can hit you'" (Kuhn, Nash, & Brucken, 1978). These stereotypes have been consistent in more recent research. When three-year-olds were asked to sort toys (e.g., a skateboard figure, a motorcycle figure, a ball and glove, an army coat, a tea set, a baby doll and crib, a ballet tutu, and a white straw hat with ribbons) into piles of "girl toys" and "boy toys," 92 percent of their responses reflected gender-typical stereotypes. By age five, the number had risen to 98 percent (Freeman, 2007). Children also show preferences for toys stereotypically associated with their own gender relative to toys associated with the other gender (Shutts, Pemberton, & Spelke, 2013). The more concrete the stereotype ("boys play with trucks" compared to "boys are good leaders"), the earlier children develop stereotypes associated with it. Later, children's stereotypes begin to incorporate personality traits and more abstract concepts. Meta-analytic work indicates that children's endorsement of gender stereotypes peaks around age six and then becomes more flexible (Signorella, Bigler, & Liben, 1993; Trautner et al., 2005).

Around age three, children start to develop the concept of gender stability, which is the understanding that boys will grow up to be men and girls will grow up to be women (Ruble et al., 2007). This is fully developed around age five, when children develop a more general sense of gender constancy, in that they believe gender is stable across time and situations (Martin et al., 2002; Ruble et al., 2007; Ruble, Balaban, & Cooper, 1981). Importantly, the age that children indicate gender consistency across situations varies tremendously across studies, often depending on how questions are asked (e.g., forced choice or open-ended) and whether a justification or explanation is expected (see Ruble et al., 2007). As children develop their understanding that gender is stable, their stereotypes become increasingly rigid; once that knowledge has been achieved, their stereotypes become more flexible.

Although gender constancy has been an important developmental milestone traditionally examined in the field of gender development, research with young transgender children highlights that there may be more nuance to children's understanding of the "constancy" of gender (Ghavami, Katsiaficas, & Rogers, 2016; Olson & Gülgöz, 2018). For example, although the gender development of transgender children is similar to cisgender children in almost all ways, including stating that most people have a stable and consistent gender identity from childhood to adulthood, young transgender children often reported that they had a different gender when they were babies (Gülgöz et al., 2019; Olson & Gülgöz, 2018). Rather than reflecting a lack of gender constancy, their responses instead reflect their own experiences, such that they were labeled one gender at birth that differs from their current gender identity. Siblings of transgender children also have a more fluid understanding of gender constancy relative to individuals without transgender siblings (e.g., saying that there are some people who change genders from childhood to adulthood; Olson & Gülgöz, 2018).

Finally, during the preschool years, many children begin to show strong preferences for their gender expression. These preferences are most visible among the more than half of young girls between the ages of three and six who boldly enter a "pink frilly dress" (PFD) phase (Halim et al., 2014). During this phase, young girls seem to internalize the gendered color-coding of pink for girls and show extreme preference for frilly pink clothing and products (Halim et al., 2014; Ruble, Lurye, & Zosuls, 2007). This phase is marked by a highly feminine appearance rigidity among girls that prioritizes appearance-focused behavior and goals, even at the expense of active and agentic movement (i.e., it is difficult to actively play in frilly dresses; Paoletti, 2012). Relatedly, girls as young as four express appearance-related concerns, such as asking for feedback on their appearance (e.g., "Does this look good on me?," "Do I look pretty?") and expressing negative comments about their appearance (e.g., "I don't like my hair/nose/bottom," "I am not pretty"; Tiggemann & Slater, 2014).

6.2.2 Socialization in Early Childhood

In early childhood, young children interact with the social world much more than they did as infants. During this developmental period, children are influenced in more substantial ways by their parents as well as their peers. A substantial body of research has documented the ways in which parents treat daughters and sons in different ways (for a review, see Brown & Tam, 2019).

One of the primary ways parents can reinforce gender stereotypes in their young children is through their encouragement of gendered play (Lytton & Romney, 1991). Parents tend to stereotype certain toys as masculine (e.g., tools and trucks) and certain toys as feminine (e.g., dolls and makeup) (Peretti & Sydney, 1984; Wood, Desmarais, & Gugula, 2002). Parents then provide their children with gendered toys, reinforce play with same-gender toys, and discourage play with cross-gender toys, regardless of children's actual toy preferences (Etaugh & Liss, 1992; Lytton & Romney, 1991; Peretti & Sydney, 1984; Raag & Rackliff, 1998; Wood et al., 2002).

There is gender asymmetry in terms of which parents are most inclined to enforce gender stereotypes, and with which children. Consistently, fathers tend to be more rigid about gender-typed play than mothers (Leaper & Friedman, 2007). Fathers are more likely to give children gender-typed toys during play than mothers and engage in rough-and-tumble play more with sons than with daughters (Bradley & Gobbart, 1989; Jacklin, DiPietro, & Maccoby, 1984). Additionally, gendered play is often more strictly enforced with sons versus daughters. Although many parents believe it is appropriate for girls to play with cross-gendered toys (e.g., girls playing with tools), many do not believe it is appropriate for boys to do the same (e.g., boys playing with a doll), and boys are less likely to receive cross-gendered toys from parents, even when they request them (Campenni, 1999; Fisher-Thompson, 1993; Robinson & Morris, 1986; Wood et al., 2002). By preschool, children recognize that parents have preferences for the types of toys they should play with, as 44 percent of preschool boys thought their fathers would say playing with girls toys was bad (Raag & Rackliff, 1998; Robinson & Morris, 1986). This recognition appears to increase across preschool. For example, whereas 20 percent of three-year-old boys thought their fathers would approve of cross-gender toy play, only 9 percent of five-year-old boys did (Freeman, 2007).

Beyond differences in play and toy choices, parents also substantially differ in how they talk to daughters and sons in early childhood. Some research has shown that parents of children in early childhood talk more with girls than boys and ask more questions to girls compared to boys (Ely, Gleason, & McCabe, 1996; Leaper et al., 1998; Vandermaas-Peeler et al., 2012). Furthermore, girls heard more diminutives and pet names, whereas boys heard more imperatives (Ely et al., 1996). The more children's parents talk to them, the more advanced their language development is (Huttenlocher et al., 1991; Tomasello, Mannle, & Kruger, 1986), and parents' tendency to talk more with girls versus boys may contribute to the later differences in language skills described in section 6.1.2.

Not only do mothers and fathers differ in the amount that they talk with girls and boys but they also differ in the topics they discuss with girls and boys. One of the most prominent differences exists in the discussion of emotion. In general, parents use a greater number and variety of emotion words when talking with daughters versus sons, especially with regards to female-typed emotions such as sadness (Adams et al., 1995; Aznar & Tenenbaum, 2015; Chaplin, Cole, & Zahn-Waxler, 2005; Maccoby, 1998; Mascaro et al., 2017). Parents are more warm, encouraging, and empathic with girls than boys and are more likely to respond to girls' displays of emotions without judgment (Chaplin et al., 2005; Fivush, 1991; Lambie & Lindberg, 2016; Mandara et al., 2012; Mascaro et al., 2017).

Although parents discuss general emotions and sadness more often with daughters, they discuss anger more often with sons (Archer, 2004; Block, 1983; Eisenberg, Cumberland, & Spinard, 1998; Letendre, 2007; Maccoby, 1998; Morris et al., 2007). Indeed, while reading stories with androgynous characters to their children, parents tended to label characters who displayed happiness or fear as female but labeled characters who displayed anger as male (van der Pol et al., 2015). Parents are also more likely to accept displays of anger and aggression from boys versus girls, and boys in turn expect less punishment for their displays of anger than girls do (Eisenberg et al., 1998; Letendre, 2007; Maccoby, 1998). Parents are also more likely to model aggression with sons versus daughters, displaying more anger and physical control (such as spanking or grabbing) toward sons than daughters (Endendijk et al., 2017; Garner, Robertson, & Smith, 1997; Kochanska et al., 2009). These gender differences in parenting may contribute to later differences in boys' and girls' displays of aggression described in section 5.1. For example, studies suggest that boys are more prone to unprovoked physical aggression than girls, while girls are more prone to relational aggression than boys (Bettencourt & Miller, 1996; Björkqvist, 2018; Crick & Grotpeter, 1995).

It is important to note that the majority of research on gender socialization has been conducted in a Westernized context, usually the United States, and there is cultural variation in these parenting patterns. Findings in some countries mimic those in the United States. For example, a study of parents and children in Spain found that mothers talk more about emotions with children than fathers and that parents talk more about emotions with girls than boys (Aznar & Tenenbaum, 2015). In a large cross-national study across fifty low- and middle-income countries, Bornstein and colleagues (2016) found that boys received moderately harsher physical punishment than girls (although physical violence was high for everyone, with 63 percent reporting physical violence and 17 percent reporting severe violence). Parents in other countries, however, display different patterns. For example, Peruvian mothers of sons use more emotion words than mothers of daughters (Melzi & Fernandez, 2004). Additionally, in one study of 868 Turkish mothers of preschool-aged children, mothers' responses to children's emotions did not differ based on child gender, except regarding sadness (Ersay, 2014). When responding to their child's sadness, mothers of boys were more likely to use magnifying responses (e.g., mimicking their sons' sadness) than mothers of girls (Ersay, 2014).

Like parents, peers also serve as an important source of gender socialization for children, and this socialization can begin as early as preschool. When children learn to label people based on gender (around age two), they begin to display a preference for same-gender peers over other-gender peers (Fagot & Leinbach, 1993; LaFreniere, Strayer, & Gauthier, 1984; Powlishta, Serbin, & Moller, 1993). This tendency leads to high degrees of gender segregation in preschools, such that preschoolers spend more time with same-gender peers, play in highly gender-segregated groups, and engage in gender-stereotypical play within those groups (Fagot, 1977; Maccoby, 1998; Martin & Fabes, 2001; Powlishta et al., 1993). Gender norms are also enforced by peers as early as preschool. Not only are children enforcing gender norms on their peers but also a majority of children engage in at least some "gender policing" or "gender enforcing." In a study of preschool children, Xiao and colleagues (2019) asked children to identify "gender enforcers" by asking them, "Who in your classroom says you shouldn't play because you are a (boy/girl)?" Results indicated that 65 percent of children were seen as gender enforcers by at least one of their peers, and the more time children spent playing with gender enforcers, the higher their gender stereotyping and gender-segregated play became over time (Xiao et al., 2019).

Research using sophisticated modeling techniques (stochastic actor-based modeling) helps elucidate the ways in which children socialize themselves in gender-segregated peers groups. Martin and colleagues (2013) conducted repeated, longitudinal observations of preschool children (enrolled in Head Start preschools in the United States) and recorded their playmates and their play activities over time. As expected, children selected same-gender play-mates and playmates with similar levels of gender-typed activities. Selection based on gender-typed activities partially mediated selection based on sex of peers. Importantly, children influenced one another's engagement in gender-typed activities over time, becoming increasingly similar to their inter-actional partners in gender-typed activities. When the investigators com-pared the mechanisms that seemed to lead to such high rates of gender segregation, they found that children were actually selecting peers more on the basis of matching gender than matching on preferred activity (Martin et al., 2013).

Beyond peers at school, schools themselves can be important sources of environmental influence. According to DIT (Bigler & Liben, 2007), when gender categorization is made salient, children increase their attention to gen-der, focusing on gender differences; this process, in turn, serves to strengthen and reinforce their gender stereotypes. Schools, especially preschools, can vary in the degree to which they make gender a salient category. Experimental research with three-to-five-year-old children in preschools involved assigning their classroom teacher to either increase or decrease the salience of gender within the classroom (Hilliard & Liben, 2010). In the high-gender-salient classrooms, teachers used gender labels in speech (e.g., "I need a girl to pass out the markers" and "Good morning boys and girls"), in their classroom organization (e.g., having separate bulletin boards for girls and boys), and in activities (e.g., lining up by girls and boys). In contrast, in the low-gender-salient classrooms, teachers were asked to avoid using gender to sort, label, and color-code children. After two weeks in these classrooms, children in the high-gender-salience classrooms, but not the low-gender-salience ones, showed stronger gender stereotypes, less positive ratings of other-gender peers, and decreased play with other-gender peers (Hilliard & Liben, 2010). Thus, simply making gender an important part of the school day led to stronger gender biases among the preschoolers.

6.3 Gender in Middle Childhood

Middle childhood (the age range of six to eleven, spanning the elementary or primary school years) is a critical period in which the academic and social foundations of later adolescence are laid. For children in middle childhood, the school context greatly informs their gender development. Gender stereotypes are often related to academic abilities, teachers at times engage in gender discrimination, and peers exert gender-conformity pressures on one another. Children in middle childhood are also avid consumers of stereotypical media that further informs their conceptions of gender.

6.3.1 Gender Development

In middle childhood, children's endorsement of gender stereotypes peaks. By age six, in US, Italian, and German samples, children endorse STEM-related gender stereotypes in favor of boys. Research relying on both explicit and implicit measures has found that both girls and boys believe that boys like math more and are better at math than girls (Cvencek et al., 2011; Muzzatti & Agnoli, 2007; Steffens, Jelenec, & Noack, 2010). Children extend those stereotypes to physics and computer science as well (Kessels, 2005; Mercier, Barron, & O'Connor, 2006). These gender differences are reflected in children's own self-concepts, such that boys, more so than girls, implicitly associate "me" and math (Cvencek et al., 2011; Steffens et al., 2010). Importantly, the more girls endorse the implicit stereotype that boys are better at math (which they endorse by about age nine), the more their own academic self-concept shifts away from math and toward languages (Steffens et al., 2010; Steffens & Jelenec, 2011).

Beyond stereotypes about boys and their greater STEM abilities, research has also shown that, by age six, girls are less likely to believe that their own gender group can be brilliant or "really, really smart" relative to boys' beliefs about their own group's brilliance (Bian, Leslie, & Cimpian, 2017). Critically, these ability beliefs are distinct from their stereotypes about who does well in school, consistent with the reality that girls often perform better than boys in school. Thus, by age six, girls are less likely to endorse the stereotype that girls are brilliant, regardless of how much better girls are doing in class, than boys are to endorse the stereotype that boys are brilliant. Furthermore, girls' lower beliefs in own-gender brilliance predicted their own diminished interest in activities described as being for children who are "really, really smart" (Bian et al., 2017). Relatedly, as boys develop an awareness that adults hold negative stereotypes about their school performance, around ages seven to eight, they, too, become susceptible to the negative effects of stereotypes (Hartley & Sutton, 2013). Taken together, this body of research indicates that children in elementary school endorse the stereotype that boys are better at STEM subjects and are more likely to be brilliant, although they do not actually perform as well in school relative to girls. For both girls and boys, these beliefs negatively predict their own preferences and performance.

Additionally, during middle childhood, children actively endorse gender stereotypes pertaining to appearance and continue endorsing stereotypes pertaining to activities. For example, when asked what being a girl means to them, one girl said, "[boys are] really nasty ... I like being a girl because girls are pretty," and another answered, "you could wear dresses, skirts, like um, and you could wear hair ties" (Rogers, 2018, p. 7). Children also express activity-focused stereotypes. When asked what it would be like if he was a girl, one boy answered, "it would be a lot different because you wouldn't be able to play football or anything" (Rogers, 2018, p. 7). Only a small percentage of children gave answers that countered gender stereotypes. For example, "I like saw a video once and it was about these girls around the world were being treated differently because they're girls and so they don't get an education because they think it's unimportant and they get enslaved or they have to get married at 13; it's really stupid" (Rogers, 2018, p. 10).

In addition to endorsing stereotypes that girls should be appearance-focused, children also seem to develop within-gender stereotypes about certain types of girls, specifically based on the degree to which they are sexualized. Across multiple studies using different stimuli (e.g., paper dolls, pictures of real girls, and videos taken from the Disney Channel), both girls and boys perceived sexualized girls (e.g., a girl wearing a mini-skirt, midriff shirt, jewelry, and makeup) to be more popular and pretty, although not as smart, nice, or athletic, than a non-sexualized girl (e.g., a girl wearing jeans and a blouse; Stone, Brown, & Jewell, 2015). Importantly, these stereotypes parallel adults' views in which both women and men perceive sexualized girls and women to be less determined, capable, and competent than non-sexualized girls and women (Daniels & Zurbriggen, 2016; Glick et al., 2005; Graff, Murnen, & Smolak, 2012). Although both girls and boys perceive sexualized girls to have high status, these stereotypes are more strongly articulated by girls than boys – perhaps because the stereotypes are applied to, and thus relevant for, girls (Stone et al., 2015).

Girls also seem to internalize aspirational images of sexualized girls (McKenney & Bigler, 2016a, 2016b). In one study of six-to-nine-year-old girls, 68.5 percent showed signs of self-sexualization and 59 percent wanted to look like a sexualized doll (Starr & Zurbriggen, 2019). Given girls' attention to sexualization and the high status conveyed to sexualized girls, it is not surprising that girls' appearance values shift away from the preschool PFDs and toward a sexualized appearance. The attention to a sexualized appearance in middle childhood appears related to children's exposure to sexualized messages from parents and media. For example, mothers' level of sexualization predicts girls' level of sexualization, and children whose mothers are more sexualized express greater appearance-related concerns (Tiggemann & Slater, 2014). Furthermore, girls who have more exposure to sexualized media endorse more positive stereotypes about sexualized girls (Stone et al., 2015), internalize sexualization messages more, and have more negative body image (Slater & Tiggemann, 2016), relative to girls with less sexualized media exposure.

Beyond endorsing gender stereotypes, children in middle childhood are aware of status differences and potential discrimination between women and men and girls and boys. Liben, Bigler, and Krogh (2001) found that, by middle childhood, children are aware of the greater status (e.g., greater income) associated with the jobs performed by men compared to jobs performed by women, even when the jobs are fictional and thus not based on actual job characteristics. Beyond knowledge of overall gender inequalities, experimental studies show that, by middle childhood, children can detect specific instances of gender discrimination from teachers in fictional stories (Brown & Bigler, 2004) and from judges in a presumably real art contest (Brown, Bigler, & Chu, 2010). When children in fourth through eighth grade (around ten years old to fourteen years old) were asked about instances of gender bias in an open-ended question (Brown et al., 2011), girls typically report that boys receive preferential treatment in athletics (e.g., "The P.E. teacher always thinks boys will be faster") and boys report that girls are given preferential treatment within the classroom (e.g., "When a girl does something wrong, the teacher never gets her in trouble. A boy does the same thing, and he always gets in trouble."). Across all ages, girls are more likely to perceive sexism than boys, perhaps reflecting their awareness of the lower social status of females relative to males (e.g., Brown & Bigler, 2004; Brown et al., 2010; Brown et al., 2011).

Finally, as children enter middle childhood, the same-gender preferences that they displayed in early childhood persist (Strough & Covatto, 2002; Zosuls et al., 2011). Children in middle childhood continue to play in highly gender-segregated peer groups, with boys playing in primarily all-boy peer groups and girls playing in smaller typically all-girl peer groups (e.g., Maccoby, 1998; Mehta & Strough, 2009). As mentioned in section 5.2, as girls and boys spend more and more of their play time interacting with same-gender peers, they increasingly socialize themselves in gender-stereotypical ways, exacerbating previously smaller differences (Mehta & Strough, 2009).

In middle childhood, more so than in early childhood, children are more likely to reject peers who display counter-stereotypical, rather than stereotype-consistent, behaviors (Blakemore, 2003; Martin, 1989). Braun and Davidson (2017) also found that elementary school children prefer gender-typical peers to gender-atypical peers, citing displays of traditionally masculine activities as reasons for liking boy classmates and a tendency to devalue feminine activities. In a study of five-to-nine-year-old children, boys gave "like" nominations to male peers who participated in sports during recess (a stereotypically masculine activity), and they gave "dislike" nominations to male peers who participated in role-play (a stereotypically feminine activity; Braza et al., 2012). In a study with Chinese four-to-nine-year-old girls and boys, children gave more positive peer appraisals (e.g., preferred being friends with and shared more stickers with) to gender-conforming compared to gender-nonconforming children in a series of vignettes (Kwan et al., 2020). This study was replicated with Canadian children and similar patterns were found, with some notable differences (Nabbijohn et al., 2020). In the Canadian sample, older children thought gender-conforming children were more well-liked, compared to gender-nonconforming children, but only for boy targets; in the Chinese sample, both girls and boys who were gender-conforming were more well-liked than gender-nonconforming children (Kwan, 2020 Nabbijohn et al., 2020). The preferences for gender-conforming children were stronger in the Chinese sample than the Canadian sample (Nabbijohn et al., 2020). These studies suggest that attitudes toward gender-nonconforming children vary, and are partially influenced, by culture. The endorsement of gender stereotypes and the rejection of noncon-forming peers are also stronger among cisgender children than transgender children (Olson & Enright, 2018).

6.3.2 Socialization in Middle Childhood

As children enter elementary school, parents continue to be an important source of gender socialization, although teachers, peers, and media begin to take on increased importance. Parents continue to show differential treatment for girls and boys, particularly based on their own stereotypes about children's academic abilities. For example, parents assume that boys like math more, need math more, and are better at math than girls (Andre et al., 1999). Parents also assume that boys are more interested in science and are better at science than girls (Tenenbaum & Leaper, 2003). Furthermore, parents attribute boys' success in math and science to innate talent, whereas they attribute girls' success to hard work (Yee & Eccles, 1988). This differential attribution occurs despite the fact that girls earn higher grades in math and science courses than boys throughout elementary school (Hill, Corbett, & St. Rose, 2010; NCES, 2013). Consistent with these stereotypes, parents are more likely to discuss numbers and science, and engage in more cognitively demanding conversations about physics, with sons than daughters (Chang, Sandhofer, & Brown, 2011; Crowley et al., 2001; Tenenbaum & Leaper, 2003). Boys report that their parents encourage involvement in science (e.g., looking at science websites together) more so than girls, and parents of girls are more likely to offer unsolicited help with math and science homework, suggesting they believe girls to be less capable in these domains (Bhanot & Jovanovic, 2005; Simpkins, Price, & Garcia, 2015).

Parental stereotypes and expectations can be even more important to children's beliefs and attitudes than actual academic experiences. For example, parents' beliefs about their children's abilities and interests affect their children's *self*-perceptions; these self-perceptions, in turn, affect children's actual performance (Gunderson et al., 2012; Jacobs, Vernon, & Eccles, 2005). Adults' beliefs about children's abilities and interests in science predict children's science self-efficacy, persistence, and competency (Tenenbaum & Leaper, 2003). In addition, parents' expectations and encouragement about computer science have been shown to be stronger predictors than children's own computer-based activities in predicting children's computer self-efficacy (Vekiri & Chronaki, 2008).

Teachers, as the other critical adults in children's lives, also hold many of the same gendered stereotypes about girls' and boys' STEM abilities as parents. Teachers often believe that boys are better at STEM subjects than girls and even underestimate girls' actual math abilities (Hand, Rice, & Greenlee, 2017; Robinson-Cimpian et al., 2014). Also like parents, teachers tend to attribute boys' STEM success to innate ability, whereas they attribute girls' success to hard work (Carlone, 2004). In contrast, although teachers perceive girls to have poorer STEM abilities than boys, they perceive girls to be more successful in school overall (Mullola et al., 2012; for a review, see Brown & Stone, 2016). Teachers rate their male students as less attentive, less persistent, and less competent than their female students, and they stereotype boys as underachieving relative to girls (Jones & Myhill, 2004; Mullola et al., 2012). Furthermore, teachers report that boys are more impulsive, more restless, and possess less effortful control than girls, even when those beliefs are unsupported by actual classroom observations (e.g., Else-Quest et al., 2006; Jones & Myhill, 2004). These beliefs are also reflected in teachers' actual behaviors, as teachers are stricter with boys than girls, and boys are more likely to be punished than girls (Pickering, 1997; Silva et al., 2015; Skiba et al., 2002). It is important to note that this disproportionate discipline is exacerbated for boys of color, particularly African American boys (e.g., Ksinan et al., 2019; Skiba et al., 2002; Wallace et al., 2008).

In interviews with girls and boys in middle childhood, it was evident that many children recognize that girls and boys are treated differently by teachers; the boys perceived differential treatment to be a form of injustice, whereas the girls blamed the boys for their own poor behavior (Myhill & Jones, 2006). Children also perceived the teachers to have different expectations for girls and boys, believing that the teachers viewed girls as needing to be treated gently but boys needing to be treated firmly.

Peers also play an important role in socializing gendered behaviors, particularly by enforcing gender conformity among one another. Although children engage in some gender policing, self-segregate into same-gender groups, and socialize themselves accordingly starting in early childhood, children in middle childhood appear more rigid in their enforcement of gender norms. Gender-atypical children are significantly more likely to be teased, rejected, and harassed than their more typical peers (Jewell & Brown, 2014; Kochel et al., 2012; Zosuls et al., 2016; Young & Sweeting, 2004). Although both girls and boys prefer gender-typical peers to atypical peers, boys are more likely to enforce gender conformity among peers. Indeed, an observational study in elementary schools found that, in the playground, high-status boys served as the gatekeepers of gender conformity and transgressions (McGuffey & Rich, 1999).

Finally, children's media is an important socializer of gender development, as there are consistent differences in how girls and boys are depicted in educational curricula, books, television, and movies. For example, in elementary school textbook depictions, females possess some masculine characteristics (such as assertiveness), but males rarely possess feminine characteristics (such as empathy; Evans & Davies, 2000). Although current television programs created for children contain more counter-stereotypical depictions of boys than in previous years (Barner, 1999; Martin, 2017), boys who are portrayed as gay or feminine are the source of jokes because of their counter-stereotypical behaviors (Myers, 2012). This trend is also evident in award-winning books prevalent in school libraries. Even among award-winning children's books considered to be nonsexist, boys never have feminine traits or occupations (Diekman & Murnen, 2004), men are rarely depicted as fathers caring for infants or children (a role usually assigned to mothers; Anderson & Hamilton, 2005), and girls are often underrepresented or portrayed with gender-stereotypical occupations (Hamilton et al., 2006).

In general, media consumed by children in middle childhood conveys two broad stereotypes: boys and men as assertive and girls and women as sexualized. For example, analyses of popular children's television programs show that boys are portrayed as answering more questions, telling others what to do more often, and showing more ingenuity than girls (Aubrey & Harrison, 2004). In video games, played more frequently by boys than girls, boys are frequently portrayed as aggressive (Dill & Thill, 2007). Boys also watch a lot of sports media (Carroll, 2005), and much of popular sports programming (such as American football and hockey) values and reinforces physical aggression and violence among men (Hardin et al., 2009; Messner, 1990; Messner & Sabo, 1994).

Media targeted to children in middle childhood also portrays girls as sexual objects. Children's television shows frequently portray girls as sexualized by wearing tight, revealing clothing (Lacroix, 2004). A study analyzing ten of the most popular television shows among European American and Latina American girls in the United States found evidence of sexualization of female characters in every show (McDade-Montez, Wallander, & Cameron, 2017). Indeed, the most common themes in popular children's shows were boys objectifying girls based on their attractiveness, as well as girls engaging in self-objectification. For example, in many children's television shows, particularly those with a male protagonist who interacts with a girl, girls are portrayed as focused on having a boyfriend and sexually objectifying themselves to attract a boy (Kirsch & Murnen, 2015). A longitudinal study with early adolescent boys found that watching mainstream television marketed to youth in late childhood/early adolescence (e.g., Disney and Nickelodeon), when coupled with gender-stereotypical parental messages, led to increases in viewing women as sex objects and viewing men as sexually dominant (Rousseau, Rodgers, & Eggermont, 2019). The sexual objectification of women is likely compounded by the use of video games, which frequently portray girls and women as sexual objects (Dill & Thill, 2007). These stereotypes are also prevalent in products marketed to girls. One-quarter of girls' clothing is revealing or has sexually suggestive writing (Goodin et al., 2011). For example, graphic tee shirts have sayings such as "Hot Stuff" printed on them in glitter letters and sweatpants have "Juicy" or "Luscious" written across the seat. Popular dolls marketed to young girls wear leather mini-skirts and thigh-high boots (e.g., Boyd & Murnen, 2017).

7 Conclusions and Future Directions

Research focused on how girls and boys develop differently and develop ideas about being a girl or boy has filled social scientific journals over the past half-century. Over that time evidence has clearly established that gender is one of the most important social groups for children, dictating whom to play with, messages they attend to, and identities they develop. Children develop stereotypes early in life, beginning in infancy, strengthening in preschool, and peaking in middle childhood before becoming more flexible in adolescence. Although their stereotypes become more flexible, these early stereotypes shape the types of play, peer groups, and academic choices children make, which all lead to long-term psychological, social, and academic consequences. Despite extensive extant research on gender development, there are still some critical areas for future research to explore, largely a result of changing cultural norms around gender.

Since the first studies of gender development, researchers have asked how much the origins and developmental trajectory of gender are based on nature versus nurture. At a fundamental level, disentangling nature from nurture has been at the core of all gender development research and is embedded in research that examines how much the pink and blue marketing of toys shapes children's toy preferences, whether classroom structure and use of gender to label and sort children increases gender stereotypes, and whether children seek out same-gender peer groups because of early differences in activity level. No doubt, contemporary developmental science appreciates that developmental systems are relational and dynamic and that development is driven by continuing transactions of individuals with their experiences. Despite this, researchers typically have an underlying assumption that either (1) gender is heavily biologically determined and gender differences are primarily due to genetic and hormonal differences between girls and boys or (2) gender is socially constructed and all gender differences are due to cultural socialization. Biological theorists have looked at the early differences between female and male infants and argued that differences that appear very early in life, before children are impacted by culture, must be (primarily) due to innate differences. Social constructionists have long asserted that gender is (primarily) meaningful to the individual because of the gender category infants are placed in at birth and the massive and ubiquitous amounts of gendered socialization that immediately follow.

The current problem, and one future research must reconcile, is that we now recognize, both scientifically and culturally, that there are many children for whom *neither* camp's explanations are satisfactory. There are millions of children who are transgender, gender-fluid, or nonbinary. For these children, their biological markers at birth (as indicated by genitalia), their gender socialization, and their own sense of gender are not neatly aligned. For many of these children, their own sense of gender develops early, is consistent across time and contexts, and is deeply felt even at great social costs (e.g., Gülgöz et al., 2019).

If developmental science is to have relevance and value, research must adapt to include *all* children (Brown, Mistry, & Yip, 2019). Therefore, current explanations for how children develop a sense of gender must be refined. Research on how children *self*-socialize in terms of their gender stereotypes, identity, and preferences may play a key role in understanding the gender development of both cisgender and transgender children (e.g., Gülgöz et al., 2019). Underlying this sentiment is the belief that children should be trusted to know their own gender, and if their experiences are not explained by existing theories, then the theories are flawed, not the children.

Given research on transgender and gender-diverse children, researchers investigating the development of gender should keep in mind the need for researching gender outside of the binary model of girls and boys (e.g., Dunham & Olson, 2016). Research has consistently demonstrated that viewing either gender or sex as a binary is inadequate. For example, research in neuroscience has found women's and men's brains are not sexually dimorphic and are more similar than they are different (Joel et al., 2015). Thus, some researchers have suggested that gender/sex be conceptualized as a categorical variable with more than two categories (Hyde et al., 2019). One option involves giving youth more than two categories to select, asking them to identify as "female," "male," "transgender female," "transgender male," "genderqueer," and "other (specify)." Another option, used by Tate and colleagues (2013), asks participants, "How do you currently identify?" and "What category were you assigned to at birth?" An additional option asks youth in an open-ended question, "What is your gender?" This allows children to use their own language and categories. Regardless of the specific measurement approach, recognizing that there may be developmental changes, researchers conducting longitudinal research must also recognize that these labels may change over time for an individual. Across these options is also the assumption that researchers should allow children to self-identify. This is highlighted by Gülgöz and colleagues (2019) who found that, although they grouped children into cisgender and transgender, these groups did not always perfectly align with the label that children gave themselves, which did not always align with children's preferred pronoun. Thus, research moving forward should carefully consider how gender is labeled and use children's own gender labels rather than ones created by the researchers.

In other words, the study of children's gender development should be conceptualized outside the binary of girls and boys and move beyond a simple comparison of gender differences. Furthermore, by studying gender in a binary way, certain populations of children, such as transgender children, intersex children, and nonbinary children are left out of the discussion. By not including diverse gender identities in research, the field cannot adequately or fully understand gender development (Dunham & Olson, 2016). For example, transgender children show different patterns of gender development only in the domain of gender consistency, compared to cisgender children (Olson & Gülgöz, 2018). Thus, using gender consistency as an important developmental milestone may no longer be appropriate or as important for development as once thought. Additionally, expanding research to include more gender-diverse children will allow for deeper theoretical understandings of gender (for a full discussion, see Dunham & Olson, 2016). For example, if an individual's gender identity does not match their sex assigned at birth, the traditional biological perspective of gender differences does not apply. Additionally, if transgender children identify as a gender other than the one their caregivers socialized them as, this indicates that social theories of gender development (e.g., Bussey & Bandura, 1999) may also not fully explain gender development. Thus, we urge future research on gender to incorporate culturally diverse and gender-diverse perspectives (Brown, Mistry, & Yip, 2019).

Beyond increasing the gender diversity of research, the current literature on gender development needs to expand its reach beyond North American and Western European samples. The majority of cross-cultural work focuses on comparing gender differences across cultures without a deeper understanding of the ways in which gender is embedded within the culture. As one example, an analysis of gender equality and academic performance across forty countries has shown that, when more women are in the labor force and have more political power, girls show better mathematics performance (Guiso et al., 2008). Research has not examined why women's participation in work is related to children's academic abilities, yet the answers can speak to how broader gender norms are transferred to children. For instance, is this relation a function of broader societal gender equality – that might also be reflected in more equitable family leave policies, greater female political representation, and equal pay – that trickles down to children and, if so, how? Is this relation related to the presence of female role models in the workforce that affects girls' academic motivation and persistence? Do certain educational practices early in schooling lead to better math performance of girls, who subsequently become the women who enter the workforce? In another example, researchers found that, in low- and middle-income countries with lower levels of gender equality, girls were less likely to work outside the home than boys, girls were more likely to be assigned excessive household chores than boys, but boys were more likely to be disadvantaged in their growth and mortality than girls (Bornstein et al., 2016). Thus, when gender equality was low, girls faced economic disadvantages, whereas boys faced physical disadvantages. Additional thoughtful research across countries can help inform *why* gender inequalities seem to persist.

In conclusion, a conscious effort to increase cross-cultural research, diversify the study of gender away from the binary, include gender-diverse identities, and connect broad social patterns to individual psychology will enrich theoretical and empirical work and is a vital component of moving the study of gender/sex forward.

References

Adams, S., Kuebli, J., Boyle, P. A., & Fivush, R. (1995). Gender differences in parent-child conversations about past emotions: A longitudinal investigation. *Sex Roles, 33*(5–6), 309–323. https://doi.org/10.1007%2FBF01954572

Alexander, G. M., Wilcox, T., & Woods, R. (2009). Sex differences in infants' visual interest in toys. *Archives of Sexual Behavior, 38*(3), 427–433.

Alink, L. R., Mesman, J., Van Zeijl, J. et al. (2006). The early childhood aggression curve: Development of physical aggression in 10- to 50-month-old children. *Child Development, 77*(4), 954–966. https://doi.org/10.1111/j.1467-8624.2006.00912.x

Anderson, D. A., & Hamilton, M. (2005). Gender role stereotyping of parents in children's picture books: The invisible father. *Sex Roles, 52*(3–4), 145–151.

Andre, T., Whigham, M., Hendrickson, A., & Chambers, S. (1999). Competency beliefs, positive affect, and gender stereotypes of elementary students and their parents about science versus other school subjects. *Journal of Research in Science Teaching, 36*(6), 719–747. 3.0.CO;2-R",1,0,0>https://doi.org/10.1002/(SICI)1098-2736(199908)36:6<719::AID-TEA8>3.0.CO;2-R

Archer, J. (2004). Sex differences in aggression in real-world settings: A meta-analytic review. *Review of General Psychology, 8*(4), 291–322. https://doi.org/10.1037/1089-2680.8.4.291

Archer, J. (2009). Does sexual selection explain human sex differences in aggression?. *Behavioral and Brain Sciences, 32*(3–4), 249–266. https://doi.org/10.1017/S0140525X09990951

Archer, J., Pearson, N. A., & Westeman, K. E. (1988). Aggressive behaviour of children aged 6–11: Gender differences and their magnitude. *British Journal of Social Psychology, 27*(4), 371–384.

Aubrey, J. S., & Harrison, K. (2004). The gender-role content of children's favorite television programs and its links to their gender-related perceptions. *Media Psychology, 6*(2), 111–146.

Auyeung, B., Baron-Cohen, S., Ashwin, E. et al. (2009). Fetal testosterone predicts sexually differentiated childhood behavior in girls and in boys. *Psychological Science, 20*(2), 144–148.

Azmitia, M., & Brown, J. R. (2002). Latino immigrant parents' beliefs about the "path of life" of their adolescent children. In J. M. Contreras, K. A. Kerns, & A. M. Neal-Barnett (Eds.), *Latino children and families in the United States: Current research and future directions* (pp. 77–105). Westport, CT: Praeger Publishers/Greenwood Publishing Group.

Aznar, A., & Tenenbaum, H. R. (2015). Gender and age differences in parent–child emotion talk. *British Journal of Developmental Psychology, 33*(1), 148–155. https://doi.org/10.1111/bjdp.12069

Baca Zinn, M., & Wells, B. (2000). Diversity within Latino families: New lessons for family social science. In D. H. Demo, K. R. Allen, & M. A. Fine (Eds.), *Handbook of family diversity* (pp. 252–273). New York: Oxford University Press.

Baillargeon, R. H., Zoccolillo, M., Keenan, K. et al. (2007). Gender differences in physical aggression: A prospective population-based survey of children before and after 2 years of age. *Developmental Psychology, 43*(1), 13–26. https://doi.org/10.1037/0012-1649.43.1.13

Barner, M. R. (1999). Sex-role stereotyping in FCC-mandated children's educational television. *Journal of Broadcasting & Electronic Media, 43*(4), 551–564.

Bem, S. L. (1981). Gender schema theory: A cognitive account of sex typing. *Psychological Review, 88*(4), 354–364. https://doi.org/10.1037/0033-295X.88.4.354

Benenson, J. F., Tennyson, R., & Wrangham, R. W. (2011). Male more than female infants imitate propulsive motion. *Cognition, 121*(2), 262–267.

Berenbaum, S. A., & Hines, M. (1992). Early androgens are related to childhood sex-typed toy preferences. *Psychological Science, 3*(3), 203–206. https://doi.org/10.1111/j.1467-9280.1992.tb00028.x

Bergelson, E., Casillas, M., Soderstrom, M., Seidl, A., Warlaumont, A. S., & Amatuni, A. (2019). What do North American babies hear? A large-scale cross-corpus analysis. *Developmental Science, 22*(1), 1-12

Bettencourt, B., & Miller, N. (1996). Gender differences in aggression as a function of provocation: A meta-analysis. *Psychological Bulletin, 119*(3), 422–447.

Bhanot, R., & Jovanovic, J. (2005). Do parents' academic gender stereotypes influence whether they intrude on their children's homework?. *Sex Roles, 52*(9–10), 597–607.

Bhanot, R. T., & Jovanovic, J. (2009). The links between parent behaviors and boys' and girls' science achievement beliefs. *Applied Developmental Science, 13*(1), 42–59.

Bian, L., Leslie, S. J., & Cimpian, A. (2017). Gender stereotypes about intellectual ability emerge early and influence children's interests. *Science, 355*(6323), 389–391.

Bigler, R. S. (1995). The role of classification skill in moderating environmental influences on children's gender stereotyping: A study of the functional use of gender in the classroom. *Child Development, 66*(4), 1072–1087.

Bigler, R. S., & Liben, L. S. (2007). Developmental Intergroup Theory. *Current Directions in Psychological Science, 16*(3), 162–166. https://doi.org/10.1111/j.1467-8721.2007.00496.x

Bigler, R. S., Spears Brown, C., & Markell, M. (2001). When groups are not created equal: Effects of group status on the formation of intergroup attitudes in children. *Child Development, 72*(4), 1151–1162.

Björkqvist, K. (2018). Gender differences in aggression. *Current Opinion in Psychology, 19*, 39–42. https://doi.org/10.1016/j.copsyc.2017.03.030

Blakemore, J. E. O. (2003). Children's beliefs about violating gender norms: Boys shouldn't look like girls, and girls shouldn't act like boys. *Sex Roles, 48* (9–10), 411–419.

Blakemore, J. E. O., Berenbaum, S. A., & Liben, L. S. (2013). *Gender development.* New York: Psychology Press.

Blakemore, J. E. O., & Centers, R. E. (2005). Characteristics of boys' and girls' toys. *Sex Roles, 53*(9–10), 619–633. https://doi.org/10.1007/s11199-005-7729-0

Block, J. H. (1983). Differential premises arising from differential socialization of the sexes: Some conjectures. *Child Development, 54*(6), 1335–1354. https://doi.org/10.2307/1129799

Bohn-Gettler, C. M., Pellegrini, A. D., Dupuis, D. et al. (2010). A longitudinal study of preschool children's (homo sapiens) sex segregation. *Journal of Comparative Psychology, 124*(2), 219–228.

Book, A. S., Starzyk, K. B., & Quinsey, V. L. (2001). The relationship between testosterone and aggression: A meta-analysis. *Aggression and Violent Behavior, 6*(6), 579–599. https://doi-org.ezproxy.uky.edu/10.1016/S1359-1789(00)00032-X

Bornstein, M. H., Arterberry, M. E., & Lamb, M. E. (2013). *Development in infancy: A contemporary introduction.* New York: Psychology Press. https://doi.org/10.4324/9780203758472

Bornstein, M. H., Hahn, C. S., & Haynes, O. M. (2004). Specific and general language performance across early childhood: Stability and gender considerations. *First Language, 24*(3), 267–304. https://doi.org/10.1177/0142723704045681

Bornstein, M. H., Putnick, D. L., Gartstein, M. A., Hahn, C. S., Auestad, N., & O'Connor, D. L. (2015). Infant temperament: Stability by age, gender, birth order, term status, and socioeconomic status. *Child Development, 86*(3), 844–863. https://doi.org/10.1111/cdev.12367

Bornstein, M. H., Putnick, D. L., Bradley, R. H., Deater-Deckard, K., & Lansford, J. E. (2016). Gender in low- and middle-income countries. *Monographs of the Society for Research in Child Development, 81*(1), 7–23.

Bos, H., & Sandfort, T. G. (2010). Children's gender identity in lesbian and heterosexual two-parent families. *Sex Roles*, *62*(1–2), 114–126.

Boyd, H., & Murnen, S. K. (2017). Thin and sexy vs. muscular and dominant: Prevalence of gendered body ideals in popular dolls and action figures. *Body Image*, *21*, 90–96.

Brachfeld-Child, S., Simpson, T., & Izenson, N. (1988). Mothers' and fathers' speech to infants in a teaching situation. *Infant Mental Health Journal*, *9*(2), 173–180.

Bradley, B. S., & Gobbart, S. K. (1989). Determinants of gender-typed play in toddlers. *The Journal of Genetic Psychology*, *150*(4), 453–455.

Braun, S. S., & Davidson, A. J. (2017). Gender (non) conformity in middle childhood: A mixed methods approach to understanding gender-typed behavior, friendship, and peer preference. *Sex Roles*, *77*(1–2), 16–29.

Braza, F., Sánchez-Martín, J. R., Braza, P. et al. (2012). Girls' and boys' choices of peer behavioral characteristics at age five. *Social Behavior and Personality: An International Journal*, *40*(10),1749–1760. https://doi.org/10.2224/sbp.2012.40.10.1749

Brown, C. S., Alabi, B., Hyunh, V., & Masten, C. (2011). Ethnicity and gender in late childhood and early adolescence: Group identity and awareness of bias. *Developmental Psychology*, *47*(2), 463–471.

Brown, C. S., & Bigler, R. S. (2002). Effects of minority status in the classroom on children's intergroup attitudes. *Journal of Experimental Child Psychology*, *83*(2), 77–110.

Brown, C. S., & Bigler, R. S. (2004). Children's perceptions of gender discrimination. *Developmental Psychology*, *40*(5), 714.

Brown, C. S., Bigler, R. S., & Chu, H. (2010). An experimental study of the correlates and consequences of perceiving oneself to be the target of gender discrimination. *Journal of Experimental Child Psychology*, *107*(2), 100–117.

Brown, C. S., Mistry, R. S., & Yip, T. (2019). Moving from the margins to the mainstream: Equity and justice as key considerations for developmental science. *Child Development Perspectives*, *13*(4), 235–240.

Brown, C. S., & Stone, E. A. (2016). Gender stereotypes and discrimination: How sexism impacts development. In S. S. Horn, M. D. Ruck, & L. S. Liben (Eds.), *Equity and justice in developmental science: Theoretical and methodological issues*, Vol. *50* (pp. 105–133). San Diego, CA: Elsevier Academic Press.

Brown, C. S., & Tam, M. J. (2019). Parenting girls and boys. In M. H. Bornstein (Ed.), *Handbook of parenting* (3rd ed.) (pp. 258–287). New York: Routledge.

Bussey, K., & Bandura, A. (1999). Social cognitive theory of gender development and differentiation. *Psychological Review*, *106*(4), 676.

Campenni, C. E. (1999). Gender stereotyping of children's toys: A comparison of parents and nonparents. *Sex Roles, 40*(1–2), 121–138.

Cancian, M., Meyer, D. R., Brown, P. R., & Cook, S. T. (2014). Who gets custody now? Dramatic changes in children's living arrangements after divorce. *Demography, 51*(4), 1381–1396.

Carlone, H. B. (2004). The cultural production of science in reform-based physics: Girls' access, participation, and resistance. *Journal of Research in Science Teaching, 41*(4), 392–414.

Carrol, J. (2005). *American public opinion about sports.* www.gallup.com/poll/15421/Sports.aspx#2

Chang, A., Sandhofer, C. M., & Brown, C. S. (2011). Gender biases in early number exposure to preschool-aged children. *Journal of Language and Social Psychology, 30*(4), 440–450.

Chaplin, T. M., & Aldao, A. (2013). Gender differences in emotion expression in children: A meta-analytic review. *Psychological Bulletin, 139*(4), 735.

Chaplin, T. M., Cole, P. M., & Zahn-Waxler, C. (2005). Parental socialization of emotion expression: Gender differences and relations to child adjustment. *Emotion, 5*(1), 80.

Condon, R. G., & Stern, P. R. (1993). Gender-role preference, gender identity, and gender socialization among contemporary Inuit youth. *Ethos, 21*(4), 384–416.

Crick, N. R., & Grotpeter, J. K. (1995). Relational aggression, gender, and social-psychological adjustment. *Child Development, 66*(3), 710–722. https://doi.org/10.1111/j.1467-8624.1995.tb00900.x

Crowley, K., Callanan, M. A., Tenenbaum, H. R., & Allen, E. (2001). Parents explain more often to boys than to girls during shared scientific thinking. *Psychological Science, 12*(3), 258–261.

Cvencek, D., Meltzoff, A. N., & Greenwald, A. G. (2011). Math–gender stereotypes in elementary school children. *Child Development, 82*(3), 766–779.

Daniels, E. A., & Zurbriggen, E. L. (2016). The price of sexy: Viewers' perceptions of a sexualized versus nonsexualized Facebook profile photograph. *Psychology of Popular Media Culture, 5*(1), 2.

Department of Health. (2004). *NHS speech and language therapy services: Summary information for 2003–2004 England.* London: Department of Health.

Diekman, A. B., & Murnen, S. K. (2004). Learning to be little women and little men: The inequitable gender equality of nonsexist children's literature. *Sex Roles, 50*(5–6), 373–385.

Dill, K. E., & Thill, K. P. (2007). Video game characters and the socialization of gender roles: Young people's perceptions mirror sexist media depictions. *Sex Roles, 57*(11–12), 851–864.

Dinella, L. M., & Weisgram, E. S. (2018). Gender-typing of children's toys: Causes, consequences, and correlates. *Sex Roles, 79*(5 6), 253–259.

Dinella, L. M., Weisgram, E. S., & Fulcher, M. (2017). Children's gender-typed toy interests: Does propulsion matter?. *Archives of Sexual Behavior, 46*(5), 1295–1305.

Domènech Rodríguez, M. M., Donovick, M. R., & Crowley, S. L. (2009). Parenting styles in a cultural context: Observations of "protective parenting" in first-generation Latinos. *Family process, 48*(2), 195–210.

Dunham, Y., & Olson, K. R. (2016). Beyond discrete categories: Studying multiracial, intersex, and transgender children will strengthen basic developmental science. *Journal of Cognition and Development, 17*(4), 642–665. https://doi.org/10.1080/15248372.2016.1195388

The Economist. (2010). The worldwide war on baby girls, *The Economist,* March 4. www.economist.com/node/15636231

Egan, S. K., & Perry, D. G. (2001). Gender identity: A multidimensional analysis with implications for psychosocial adjustment. *Developmental Psychology, 37*(4), 451.

Eichstedt, J. A., Serbin, L. A., Poulin-Dubois, D., & Sen, M. G. (2002). Of bears and men: Infants' knowledge of conventional and metaphorical gender stereotypes. *Infant Behavior and Development, 25*(3), 296–310.

Eisenberg, N., Cumberland, A., & Spinrad, T. L. (1998). Parental socialization of emotion. *Psychological Inquiry, 9*(4), 241–273.

Else-Quest, N. M., Hyde, J. S., Goldsmith, H. H., & Van Hulle, C. A. (2006). Gender differences in temperament: A meta-analysis. *Psychological Bulletin, 132*(1), 33.

Ely, R., Gleason, J. B., & McCabe, A. (1996). "Why didn't you talk to your mommy, honey?": Parents' and children's talk about talk. *Research on Language and Social Interaction, 29*(1), 7–25.

Endendijk, J. J., Groeneveld, M. G., van der Pol, L. D. et al. (2017). Gender differences in child aggression: Relations with gender-differentiated parenting and parents' gender-role stereotypes. *Child Development, 88*(1), 299–316.

Ersay, E. (2014). Parental socialization of emotion: How mothers respond to their children's emotions in Turkey. *International Journal of Emotional Education, 6*(1), 33–46. http://ezproxy.uky.edu/login?url=https://search-pro quest-com.ezproxy.uky.edu/docview/1526112392?accountid=11836

Etaugh, C., & Liss, M. B. (1992). Home, school, and playroom: Training grounds for adult gender roles. *Sex Roles, 26*(3–4), 129–147.

European Union for Gender Equality. (2019). *Gender Equality Index.* https:// eige.europa.eu/publications/gender-equality-index-2019-brief-still-far-fin ish-line

Evans, L., & Davies, K. (2000). No sissy boys here: A content analysis of the representation of masculinity in elementary school reading textbooks. *Sex Roles, 42*(3–4), 255–270.

Fabes, R. A., Hanish, L. D., & Martin, C. L. (2003). Children at play: The role of peers in understanding the effects of child care. *Child Development, 74*(4), 1039–1043.

Fagot, B. I. (1977). Consequences of moderate cross-gender behavior in preschool children. *Child Development, 48*(3), 902–907. https://doi.org/10.2307/1128339

Fagot, B. I., & Leinbach, M. D. (1993). Gender-role development in young children: From discrimination to labeling. *Developmental Review, 13*(2), 205–224. https://doi.org/10.1006/drev.1993.1009

Farr, R. H. (2016). Review of Adoption by lesbians and gay men: A new dimension in family diversity. *Journal of Family Theory & Review, 8*(1), 121–127.

Farr, R. H., Bruun, S. T., Doss, K. M., & Patterson, C. J. (2018). Children's gender-typed behavior from early to middle childhood in adoptive families with lesbian, gay, and heterosexual parents. *Sex Roles, 78*(7–8), 528–541.

Farr, R. H., Forssell, S. L., & Patterson, C. J. (2010). Parenting and child development in adoptive families: Does parental sexual orientation matter?. *Applied Developmental Science, 14*(3), 164–178.

Fast, A. A., & Olson, K. R. (2018). Gender development in transgender preschool children. *Child Development, 89*(2), 620–637.

Fisher-Thompson, D. (1993). Adult toy purchases for children: Factors affecting sex-typed toy selection. *Journal of Applied Developmental Psychology, 14*(3), 385–406.

Fivush, R. (1991). Gender and emotion in mother-child conversations about the past. *Journal of Narrative and Life History, 1*(4), 325–341.

Freeman, N. K. (2007). Preschoolers' perceptions of gender appropriate toys and their parents' beliefs about genderized behaviors: Miscommunication, mixed messages, or hidden truths?. *Early Childhood Education Journal, 34*(5), 357–366.

Fulcher, M., & Hayes, A. R. (2018). Building a pink dinosaur: The effects of gendered construction toys on girls' and boys' play. *Sex Roles, 79*(5–6), 273–284.

Garcia, S. E. (2019). Explosion at gender reveal party kills woman, officials say. *New York Times*, October 28. www.nytimes.com/2019/10/28/us/gender-reveal-party-death.html.

Garner, P. W., Robertson, S., & Smith, G. (1997). Preschool children's emotional expressions with peers: The roles of gender and emotion socialization. *Sex Roles, 36*(11–12), 675–691.

Gates, G. J. (2015). Marriage and family: LGBT individuals and same-sex couples. *The Future of Children, 25*(2), 67–87.

Ghavami, N., Katsiaficas, D., & Rogers, L. O. (2016). Toward an intersectional approach in developmental science: The role of race, gender, sexual orientation, and immigrant status. In S. S. Horn, M. D. Ruck, & L. S. Liben (Eds.), *Equity and justice in developmental science: Theoretical and methodological issues, Vol. 1* (pp. 31–73). San Diego, CA: Elsevier Academic Press. https://doi.org/10.1016/bs.acdb.2015.12.001

Gil, R. M., & Vazquez, C. I. (1996). *The Maria paradox: How Latinas can merge old world traditions with new world self esteem.* New York: Putnam's Sons.

Gilkerson, J., Richards, J. A., & Topping, K. J. (2017). The impact of book reading in the early years on parent–child language interaction. *Journal of Early Childhood Literacy, 17*(1), 92–110.

Glick, P., Larsen, S., Johnson, C., & Branstiter, H. (2005). Evaluations of sexy women in low-and high-status jobs. *Psychology of Women Quarterly, 29*(4), 389–395.

Goodin, S. M., Van Denburg, A., Murnen, S. K., & Smolak, L. (2011). "Putting on" sexiness: A content analysis of the presence of sexualizing characteristics in girls' clothing. *Sex Roles, 65*(1–2), 1–12.

Graff, K., Murnen, S. K., & Smolak, L. (2012). Too sexualized to be taken seriously? Perceptions of a girl in childlike vs. sexualizing clothing. *Sex Roles, 66*(11–12), 764–775.

Guiso, L., Monte, F., Sapienza, P., & Zingales, L. (2008). Culture, gender, and math. *Science, 320*(5880), 1164.

Gülgöz, S., Glazier, J. J., Enright, E. A. et al. (2019). Similarity in transgender and cisgender children's gender development. *Proceedings of the National Academy of Sciences, 116*(49), 24480–24485. https://doi.org/10.1073/pnas.1909367116

Gunderson, E. A., Ramirez, G., Levine, S. C., & Beilock, S. L. (2012). The role of parents and teachers in the development of gender-related math attitudes. *Sex Roles, 66*(3–4), 153–166.

Halim, M. L., Ruble, D. N., Tamis-LeMonda, C. S., Zosuls, K. M., Lurye, L. E., & Greulich, F. K. (2014). Pink frilly dresses and the avoidance of all things "girly": Children's appearance rigidity and cognitive theories of gender development. *Developmental Psychology, 50*(4), 1091–1101. https://doi.org/10.1037/a0034906.supp

Hamilton, M. C., Anderson, D., Broaddus, M., & Young, K. (2006). Gender stereotyping and under-representation of female characters in 200 popular children's picture books: A twenty-first century update. *Sex Roles, 55*(11–12), 757–765.

Hammer, C. S., Farkas, G., & Maczuga, S. (2010). The language and literacy development of Head Start children: A study using the Family and Child Experiences Survey database. *Language, Speech, and Hearing Services in Schools*, *41*(1), 70–83.

Hand, S., Rice, L., & Greenlee, E. (2017). Exploring teachers' and students' gender role bias and students' confidence in STEM fields. *Social Psychology of Education: An International Journal*, *20*(4), 929–945. https://doi.org/10.1007/s11218-017-9408-8

Hardin, M., Kuehn, K. M., Jones, H., Genovese, J., & Balaji, M. (2009). "Have you got game?": Hegemonic masculinity and neo-homophobia in US newspaper sports columns. *Communication, Culture & Critique*, *2*(2), 182–200.

Hartley, B. L., & Sutton, R. M. (2013). A stereotype threat account of boys' academic underachievement. *Child Development*, *84*(5), 1716–1733.

Hay, D. F. (2017). The early development of human aggression. *Child Development Perspectives*, *11*(2), 102–106. https://doi.org/10.1111/cdep.12220

Hay, D. F., Nash, A., Caplan, M., Swartzentruber, J., Ishikawa, F., & Vespo, J. E. (2011). The emergence of gender differences in physical aggression in the context of conflict between young peers. *British Journal of Developmental Psychology*, *29*(2), 158–175. https://doi.org/10.1111/j.2044-835X.2011.02028.x

Hill, C., Corbett, C., & St Rose, A. (2010). *Why so few? Women in science, technology, engineering, and mathematics*. Washington, DC: American Association of University Women.

Hilliard, L. J., & Liben, L. S. (2010). Differing levels of gender salience in preschool classrooms: Effects on children's gender attitudes and intergroup bias. *Child Development*, *81*(6), 1787–1798.

Hondagneu-Sotelo, P. (1994). *Gendered transitions: Mexican experiences of immigration. Berkeley: University of* California Press.

Huttenlocher, J., Haight, W., Bryk, A., Seltzer, M., & Lyons, T. (1991). Early vocabulary growth: Relation to language input and gender. *Developmental Psychology*, *27*(2), 236–248.

Hyde, J. S. (1984). How large are gender differences in aggression? A developmental meta-analysis. *Developmental Psychology*, *20*(4),722–736. https://doi.org/10.1037/0012-1649.20.4.722

Hyde, J. S. (2005). The gender similarities hypothesis. *American Psychologist*, *60*(6), 581–592. https://doi.org/10.1037/0003-066X.60.6.581

Hyde, J. S., Bigler, R. S., Joel, D., Tate, C. C., & van Anders, S. M. (2019). The future of sex and gender in psychology: Five challenges to the gender binary. *American Psychologist*, *74*(2), 171–193. https://doi.org/10.1037/amp0000307

Hyde, J. S., Fennema, E., & Lamon, S. J. (1990). Gender differences in mathematics performance: A meta-analysis. *Psychological Bulletin*, *107*(2), 139–155. https://doi.org/10.1037/0033-2909.107.2.139

Hyde, J. S., Lindberg, S. M., Linn, M. C., Ellis, A. B., & Williams, C. C. (2008). Gender similarities characterize math performance. *Science*, *321*(5888), 494–495.

Jacklin, C. N., DiPietro, J. A., and Maccoby, E. E. (1984). Sex-typing behavior and sex-typing pressure in child/parent interaction. *Archives of Sexual Behavior*, *13*(5), 413–425. https://doi.org/10.1007/BF01541427

Jacobs, J. E., Vernon, M. K., & Eccles, J. S. (2005). Activity choices in middle childhood: The roles of gender, self-beliefs, and parents' influence. In J. L. Mahoney, R. W. Larson, & J. S. Eccles (Eds.), *Organized activities as contexts of development: Extracurricular activities, after-school and community programs* (pp. 235–254). Mahwah, NJ: Lawrence Erlbaum Associates.

Jewell, J. A., & Brown, C. S. (2014). Relations among gender typicality, peer relations, and mental health during early adolescence. *Social Development*, *23*(1), 137–156.

Joel, D., Berman, Z., Tavor, I. et al. (2015). Sex beyond the genitalia: The human brain mosaic. *Proceedings of the National Academy of Sciences*, *112*(50), 15468–15473. https://doi.org/10.1073/pnas.1509654112

Johnson, K., Caskey, M., Rand, K., Tucker, R., & Vohr, B. (2014). Gender differences in adult-infant communication in the first months of life. *Pediatrics*, *134*(6), e1603–e1610.

Jones, S., & Myhill, D. (2004). "Troublesome boys" and "compliant girls": Gender identity and perceptions of achievement and underachievement. *British Journal of Sociology of Education*, *25*(5), 547–561. https://doi.org/10.1080/0142569042000252044

Jordan-Young, R., & Rumiati, R. I. (2012). Hardwired for sexism? Approaches to sex/gender in neuroscience. *Neuroethics*, *5*(3), 305–315.

Kersey, A. J., Braham, E. J., Csumitta, K. D., Libertus, M. E., & Cantlon, J. F. (2018). No intrinsic gender differences in children's earliest numerical abilities. *npj Science of Learning*, *3*(1), 1–10. https://doi.org/10.1038/s41539-018-0028-7

Kessels, U. (2005). Fitting into the stereotype: How gender-stereotyped perceptions of prototypic peers relate to liking for school subjects. *European Journal of Psychology of Education*, *20*(3), 309–323. https://doi.org/10.1007/BF03173559

Kirsch, A. C., & Murnen, S. K. (2015). "Hot" girls and "cool dudes": Examining the prevalence of the heterosexual script in American children's television media. *Psychology of Popular Media Culture, 4*(1), 18–30.

Knickmeyer, R. C., Wheelwright, S., Taylor, K., Raggatt, P., Hackett, G., & Baron-Cohen, S. (2005). Gender-typed play and amniotic testosterone. *Developmental Psychology, 41*(3), 517.

Knight, G. P., Guthrie, I. K., Page, M. C., & Fabes, R. A. (2002). Emotional arousal and gender differences in aggression: A meta-analysis. *Aggressive Behavior: Official Journal of the International Society for Research on Aggression, 28*(5), 366–393.

Kochanska, G., Barry, R. A., Stellern, S. A., & O'bleness, J. J. (2009). Early attachment organization moderates the parent–child mutually coercive pathway to children's antisocial conduct. *Child Development, 80*(4), 1288–1300.

Kochel, K. P., Miller, C. F., Updegraff, K. A., Ladd, G. W., & Kochenderfer-Ladd, B. (2012). Associations between fifth graders' gender atypical problem behavior and peer relationships: A short-term longitudinal study. *Journal of Youth and Adolescence, 41*(8), 1022–1034.

Kohlberg, L. (1966). A cognitive-developmental analysis of children's sex-role concepts and attitudes. In E. E. Maccoby (Ed.), *The development of sex differences* (pp. 82–173). Stanford: Stanford University Press.

Ksinan, A. J., Vazsonyi, A. T., Ksinan, G., & Peugh, J. L. (2019). National ethnic and racial disparities in disciplinary practices : A contextual analysis in American secondary schools. *Journal of School Psychology, 74*(March), 106–125. https://doi.org/10.1016/j.jsp.2019.05.003

Kuhn, D., Nash, S. C., & Brucken, L. (1978). Sex role concepts of two-and three-year-olds. *Child Development, 49*(2), 445–451.

Kung, K. T. F., Browne, W. V., Constantinescu, M., Noorderhaven, R. M., & Hines, M. (2016). Early postnatal testosterone predicts sex-related differences in early expressive vocabulary. *Psychoneuroendocrinology, 68*, 111–116. https://doi.org/10.1016/j.psyneuen.2016.03.001

Kwan, K. M. W., Shi, S. Y., Nabbijohn, A. N., MacMullin, L. N., VanderLaan, D. P., & Wong, W. I. (2020). Children's appraisals of gender nonconformity: Developmental pattern and intervention. *Child Development, 91*(4), e780–e798.

Lacroix, C. (2004). Images of animated others: The orientalization of Disney's cartoon heroines from The Little Mermaid to The Hunchback of Notre Dame. *Popular Communication, 2*(4), 213–229.

LaFreniere, P., Strayer, F. F., & Gauthier, R. (1984). The emergence of same-sex affiliative preferences among preschool peers: A developmental/ethological perspective. *Child Development, 55*(5), 1958–1965. https://doi.org/10.2307/1129942

Lambie, J. A., & Lindberg, A. (2016). The role of maternal emotional validation and invalidation on children's emotional awareness. *Merrill-Palmer Quarterly, 62*(2), 129–157.

Leaper, C. (2015). Gender and social-cognitive development. In L. S. Liben, U. Müller, R. M. Lerner, L. S. Liben, U. Müller, & R. M. Lerner (Eds.), *Handbook of child psychology and developmental science: Cognitive processes*, Vol. 2 (7th ed., pp. 806–853). Hoboken, NJ: John Wiley and Sons.

Leaper, C., Anderson, K. J., & Sanders, P. (1998). Moderators of gender effects on parents' talk to their children: A meta-analysis. *Developmental Psychology, 34*(1), 3–27.

Leaper, C., & Ayres, M. M. (2007). A meta-analytic review of gender variations in adults' language use: Talkativeness, affiliative speech, and assertive speech. *Personality and Social Psychology Review, 11*(4), 328–363.

Leaper, C., & Friedman, C. K. (2007). The socialization of gender. In J. E. Grusec & P. D. Hastings (Eds.), *Handbook of socialization: Theory and research* (pp. 561–587). New York: Guilford Press.

Leaper, C., & Smith, T. E. (2004). A meta-analytic review of gender variations in children's language use: Talkativeness, affiliative speech, and assertive speech. *Developmental Psychology, 40*(6), 993–1027.

Leinbach, M. D., & Fagot, B. I. (1986). Acquisition of gender labels: A test for toddlers. *Sex Roles, 15*(11–12), 655–666.

Leinbach, M. D., & Fagot, B. I. (1993). Categorical habituation to male and female faces: Gender schematic processing in infancy. *Infant Behavior and Development, 16*(3), 317–332. https://doi.org/10.1016/0163-6383(93)80038-A

Letendre, J. (2007). "Sugar and spice but not always nice": Gender socialization and its impact on development and maintenance of aggression in adolescent girls. *Child and Adolescent Social Work Journal, 24*(4), 353–368. https://doi.org/10.1007/s10560-007-0088-7

Levy, G. D. (1999). Gender-typed and non-gender-typed category awareness in toddlers. *Sex Roles, 41*(11–12), 851–873. https://doi.org/10.1023/A:1018832529622

Levy, G. D., & Haaf, R. A. (1994). Detection of gender-related categories by 10-month-old infants. *Infant Behavior and Development, 17*(4), 457–459. https://doi.org/10.1016/0163-6383(94)90037-X

Liben, L. S., Bigler, R. S., & Krogh, H. R. (2001). Pink and blue collar jobs: Children's judgments of job status and job aspirations in relation to sex of worker. *Journal of Experimental Child Psychology, 79*(4), 346–363.

Lindberg, S. M., Hyde, J. S., Petersen, J. L., & Linn, M. C. (2010). New trends in gender and mathematics performance: A meta-analysis. *Psychological Bulletin, 136*(6), 1123–1135.

Loeber, R., Capaldi, D. M., & Costello, E. (2013). Gender and the development of aggression, disruptive behavior, and delinquency from childhood to early adulthood. In P. H. Tolan & B. L. Leventhal (Eds.), *Disruptive behavior disorders* (pp. 137–160). New York: Springer.

Love, J. A., & Buriel, R. (2007). Language brokering, autonomy, parent-child bonding, biculturalism, and depression: A study of Mexican American adolescents from immigrant families. *Hispanic Journal of Behavioral Sciences, 29*(4), 472–491.

Lytton, H., & Romney, D.M. (1991). Parents' differential socialization of boys and girls: A meta-analysis. *Psychological Bulletin, 109*(2), 267–296. https://doi.org/10.1037/0033-2909.109.2.267

Maccoby, E. E. (1966). *The development of sex differences*. Stanford: Stanford University Press.

Maccoby, E. E. (1998). *The two sexes: Growing up apart, coming together.* Cambridge, MA: Harvard University Press.

Maccoby, E. E., & Jacklin, C. N. (1974). *The psychology of sex differences.* Stanford: Stanford University Press.

Maccoby, E. E., & Jacklin, C. N. (1987). Gender segregation in childhood. In H. W. Reese (Ed.), *Advances in child development and behavior*, Vol. *20* (pp. 239–287). San Diego, CA: Academic Press.

MacPhee, D., & Prendergast, S. (2019). Room for improvement: Girls' and boys' home environments are still gendered. *Sex Roles, 80*(5–6), 332–346. https://doi.org/10.1007/s11199-018-0936-2

Mandara, J., Murray, C. B., Telesford, J. M., Varner, F. A., & Richman, S. B. (2012). Observed gender differences in African American mother-child relationships and child behavior. *Family Relations, 61*(1), 129–141.

Martin, R. (2017). Gender and emotion stereotypes in children's television. *Journal of Broadcasting & Electronic Media, 61*(3), 499–517.

Martin, C. L. (1989). Children's use of gender-related information in making social judgments. *Developmental Psychology, 25*(1), 80.

Martin, C. L., Andrews, N. C., England, D. E., Zosuls, K., & Ruble, D. N. (2017). A dual identity approach for conceptualizing and measuring children's gender identity. *Child Development, 88*(1), 167–182. https://doi.org/10.1111/cdev.12568

Martin, C. L., Eisenbud, L., & Rose, H. (1995). Children's gender-based reasoning about toys. *Child Development, 66*(5), 1453–1471. https://doi.org/10.1111/j.1467-8624.1995.tb00945.x

Martin, C. L., & Fabes, R. A. (2001). The stability and consequences of young children's samesex peer interactions. *Developmental Psychology, 37*(3), 431–446. https://doi.org/10.1037/0012-1649.37.3.431

Martin, C. L., Fabes, R. A., Hanish, L., Leonard, S., & Dinella, L. M. (2011). Experienced and expected similarity to same-gender peers: Moving toward a comprehensive model of gender segregation. *Sex Roles*, *65*(5–6), 421–434.

Martin, C. L., & Halverson, C. F., Jr. (1983). The effects of sex-typing schemas on young children's memory. *Child Development*, *54*(3), 563–574. www .jstor.org/stable/1130043

Martin, C. L., Kornienko, O., Schaefer, D. R., Hanish, L. D., Fabes, R. A., & Goble, P. (2013). The role of sex of peers and gender-typed activities in young children's peer affiliative networks: A longitudinal analysis of selection and influence. *Child Development*, *84*(3), 921–937.

Martin, C. L., & Ruble, D. N. (2010). Patterns of gender development. *Annual Review of Psychology*, *61*(1), 353–381. https://doi.org/10.1146/annurev .psych.093008.100511

Martin, C. L., Ruble, D. N., & Szkrybalo, J. (2002). Cognitive theories of early gender development. *Psychological Bulletin*, *128*(6), 903–933. https://doi .org/10.1037/0033-2909.128.6.903

Mascaro, J. S., Rentscher, K. E., Hackett, P. D., Mehl, M. R., & Rilling, J. K. (2017). Child gender influences paternal behavior, language, and brain function. *Behavioral Neuroscience*, *131*(3), 262–273. https://doi.org/10 .1037%2Fbne0000199

McDade-Montez, E., Wallander, J., & Cameron, L. (2017). Sexualization in US Latina and White girls' preferred children's television programs. *Sex Roles*, *77*(1–2), 1–15.

McGuffey, C. S., & Rich, B. L. (1999). Playing in the gender transgression zone: Race, class, and hegemonic masculinity in middle childhood. *Gender & Society*, *13*(5), 608–627.

McHale, S. M., Crouter, A. C., & Tucker, C. J. (1999). Family context and gender role socialization in middle childhood: Comparing girls to boys and sisters to brothers. *Child Development*, *70*(4), 990–1004.

McKenney, S. J., & Bigler, R. S. (2016a). High heels, low grades: Internalized sexualization and academic orientation among adolescent girls. *Journal of Research on Adolescence*, *26*(1), 30–36.

McKenney, S. J., & Bigler, R. S. (2016b). Internalized sexualization and its relation to sexualized appearance, body surveillance, and body shame among early adolescent girls. *The Journal of Early Adolescence*, *36*(2), 171–197.

Mehta, C. M., & Strough, J. (2009). Sex segregation in friendships and normative contexts across the life span. *Developmental Review*, *29*(3), 201–220. https://doi.org/10.1016/j.dr.2009.06.001

Melzi, G., & Fernández, C. (2004). Talking about past emotions: Conversations between Peruvian mothers and their preschool children. *Sex Roles, 50*(9–10), 641–657. https://doi.org/10.1023%2FB%3ASERS.0000027567.55262.10

Mercier, E. M., Barron, B., & O'connor, K. M. (2006). Images of self and others as computer users: The role of gender and experience. *Journal of Computer Assisted Learning, 22*(5), 335–348.

Merz, E. C., Zucker, T. A., Landry, S. H. et al. (2015). Parenting predictors of cognitive skills and emotion knowledge in socioeconomically disadvantaged preschoolers. *Journal of Experimental Child Psychology, 132*, 14–31. https://doi.org/10.1016/j.jecp.2014.11.010

Messner, M. A. (1990). When bodies are weapons: Masculinity and violence in sport. *International Review for the Sociology of Sport, 25*(3), 203–220. https://doi.org/10.1177/101269029002500303

Messner, M. A., & Sabo, D. F. (1994). *Sex, violence & power in sports: Rethinking masculinity.* Freedom, CA: The Crossing Press.

Miller, C. L. (1983). Developmental changes in male/female voice classification by infants. *Infant Behavior and Development, 6*(2–3), 313–330. https://doi.org/10.1016/S0163-6383(83)80040-X

Mischel, W. (1966). A social learning view of sex differences in behavior. In E. Maccoby (Ed.), *The development of sex differences* (pp. 57–81). Stanford: Stanford University Press.

Mondschein, E. R., Adolph, K. E., & Tamis-LeMonda, C. S. (2000). Gender bias in mothers' expectations about infant crawling. *Journal of Experimental Child Psychology, 77*(4),304–316. https://doi.org/10.1006/jecp.2000.2597

Morris, A. S., Silk, J. S., Steinberg, L., Myers, S. S., & Robinson, L. R. (2007). The role of the family context in the development of emotion regulation. *Social Development, 16*(2), 361–388.

Muehlenhard, C. L., & Peterson, Z. D. (2011). Distinguishing between sex and gender: History, current conceptualizations, and implications. *Sex Roles, 64*(11–12), 791–803. https://doi.org/10.1007/s11199-011-9932-5

Mullola, S., Ravaja, N., Lipsanen, J. et al. (2012). Gender differences in teachers' perceptions of students' temperament, educational competence, and teachability. *British Journal of Educational Psychology, 82*(2), 185–206. https://doi.org/10.1111/j.2044-8279.2010.02017.x

Muzzatti, B., & Agnoli, F. (2007). Gender and mathematics: Attitudes and stereotype threat susceptibility in Italian children. *Developmental Psychology, 43*(3), 747–759.

Myers, K. (2012). "Cowboy up!": Non-hegemonic representations of masculinity in children's television programming. *The Journal of Men's Studies, 20*(2), 125–143.

Myhill, D., & Jones, S. (2006). "She doesn't shout at no girls": Pupils' perceptions of gender equity in the classroom. *Cambridge Journal of Education, 36*(1), 99–113. https://doi.org/10.1080/03057640500491054

Nabbijohn, A. N., MacMullin, L. N., Kwan, K. M. W. et al. (2020). Children's bias in appraisals of gender-variant peers. *Journal of Experimental Child Psychology, 196*, 1–10. https://doi.org/10.1016/j.jecp.2020.104865

NCES (National Center for Education Statistics). (2013). *The condition of education.* Washington, DC: US Department of Education. http://nces.ed.gov/pubsearch

Nivette, A. E., Eisner, M., Malti, T., & Ribeaud, D. (2014). Sex differences in aggression among children of low and high gender inequality backgrounds: A comparison of gender role and sexual selection theories. *Aggressive Behavior, 40*(5), 451–464. https://doi.org/10.1002/ab.21530

Ocha, W. (2012). Transsexual emergence: Gender variant identities in Thailand. *Culture, Health & Sexuality, 14*(5), 563–575.

OECD (2015), *Education at a glance 2015: OECD indicators.* Paris: OECD Publishing. https://doi.org/10.1787/eag-2015-en

Olson, K. R., Durwood, L., DeMeules, M., & McLaughlin, K. A. (2016). Mental health of transgender children who are supported in their identities. *Pediatrics, 137*(3), 1–8.

Olson, K. R., & Enright, E. A. (2018). Do transgender children (gender) stereotype less than their peers and siblings?. *Developmental Science, 21*(4), 1–12.

Olson, K. R., & Gülgöz, S. (2018). Early findings from the TransYouth Project: Gender development in transgender children. *Child Development Perspectives, 12*(2), 93–97. https://doi.org/10.1111/cdep.12268

Paoletti, J. B. (2012). *Pink and blue: Telling the boys from the girls in America.* Bloomington: Indiana University Press.

Pasterski, V. L., Geffner, M. E., Brain, C., Hindmarsh, P., Brook, C., & Hines, M. (2005). Prenatal hormones and postnatal socialization by parents as determinants of male-typical toy play in girls with congenital adrenal hyperplasia. *Child Development, 76*(1), 264–278. https://doi.org/10.1111/j.1467-8624.2005.00843.x

Peretti, P. O., & Sydney, T. M. (1984). Parental toy choice stereotyping and its effects on child toy preference and sex-role typing. *Social Behavior and Personality: An International Journal, 12*(2), 213–216.

Phinney, J. S. (1990). Ethnic identity in adolescents and adults: Review of research. *Psychological Bulletin, 108*(3), 499–514.

Pickering, J. (1997). *Raising boys' achievement.* London: A&C Black.

Pomerleau, A., Bolduc, D., Malcuit, G., & Cossette, L. (1990). Pink or blue: Environmental gender stereotypes in the first two years of life. *Sex Roles, 22*(5–6), 359–367. https://doi.org/10.1007/BF00288339

Poulin-Dubois, D., Serbin, L. A., & Derbyshire, A. (1998). Toddlers' intermodal and verbal knowledge about gender. *Merrill-Palmer Quarterly, 44*(*3*), 338–354.

Poulin-Dubois, D., Serbin, L. A., Kenyon, B., & Derbyshire, A. (1994). Infants' intermodal knowledge about gender. *Developmental Psychology, 30*(3), 436–442.

Powlishta, K. K., Serbin, L. A., & Moller, L. C. (1993). The stability of individual differences in gender typing: Implications for understanding gender segregation. *Sex Roles, 29*(11–12), 723–737. https://doi.org/10.1007/BF00289214

Quinn, P. C., Yahr, J., Kuhn, A., Slater, A. M., & Pascalis, O. (2002). Representation of the gender of human faces by infants: A preference for female. *Perception, 31*(9), 1109–1121. https://doi.org/10.1068/p3331

Raag, T., & Rackliff, C. L. (1998). Preschoolers' awareness of social expectations of gender: Relationships to toy choices. *Sex Roles, 38*(9–10), 685–700.

Raffaelli, M., & Ontai, L. L. (2004). Gender socialization in Latino/a families: Results from two retrospective studies. *Sex Roles, 50*(5–6), 287–299.

Ramsey, J. L., Langlois, J. H., & Marti, C. N. (2005). Infant categorization of faces: Ladies first. *Developmental Review, 25*, 212–246.

Ramsey-Rennels, J. L., & Langlois, J. H. (2006). Infants' differential processing of female and male faces. *Current Directions in Psychological Science, 15*(2), 59–62.

Rheingold, H. L., & Cook, K. V. (1975). The content of boys' and girls' rooms as an index of parents' behavior. *Child Development, 46*, 459–463. https://doi.org/10.2307/1128142.

Rider, G. N., McMorris, B. J., Gower, A. L., Coleman, E., & Eisenberg, M. E. (2018). Health and care utilization of transgender and gender nonconforming youth: A population-based study. *Pediatrics, 141*(3), 1–8.

Robinson, C. C., & Morris, J. T. (1986). The gender-stereotyped nature of Christmas toys received by 36-, 48-, and 60-month-old children: A comparison between nonrequested vs requested toys. *Sex Roles, 15*(1–2), 21–32.

Robinson-Cimpian, J. P., Lubienski, S. T., Ganley, C. M., & Copur-Gencturk, Y. (2014). Teachers' perceptions of students' mathematics proficiency may exacerbate early gender gaps in achievement. *Developmental Psychology, 50*(4), 1262–1281. https://doi.org/10.1037/a0035073

Rogers, L. O. (2018). "i'm kind of a feminist": Using master narratives to analyze gender identity in middle childhood. *Child Development, 91*(1), 179–196. https://doi.org/10.1111/cdev.13142

Rousseau, A., Rodgers, R. F., & Eggermont, S. (2019). A short-term longitudinal exploration of the impact of TV exposure on objectifying attitudes toward women in early adolescent boys. *Sex Roles, 80*(3–4), 186–199.

Ruble, D. N., Balaban, T., & Cooper, J. (1981). Gender constancy and the effects of sex-typed televised toy commercials. *Child Development, 52*(2), 667–673.

Ruble, D. N., Lurye, L. E., & Zosuls, K. M. (2007). Pink frilly dresses (PFD) and early gender identity. *Princeton Report on Knowledge, 2*(2).

Ruble, D. N., & Martin, C. L. (1998). Gender development. In N. Eisenberg (Ed.), *Handbook of child psychology, Vol. 3: Social, emotional, and personality development* (pp. 933–1016). New York: Wiley.

Ruble, D. N., Martin, C. L., & Berenbaum, S. A. (2006). Gender development. In N. Eisenberg, W. Damon, & R. M. Lerner (Eds.), *Handbook of child psychology: Social, emotional, and personality development*, Vol. 3 (6th ed., pp. 858–932). Hoboken, NJ: John Wiley & Sons.

Ruble, D. N., Taylor, L. J., Cyphers, L., Greulich, F. K., Lurye, L. E., & Shrout, P. E. (2007). The role of gender constancy in early gender development. *Child Development, 78*(4), 1121–1136.

Sandberg, D. E., Meyer-Bahlburg, H. F., Ehrhardt, A. A., & Yager, T. J. (1993). The prevalence of gender-atypical behavior in elementary school children. *Journal of the American Academy of Child & Adolescent Psychiatry, 32*(2), 306–314. https://doi.org/10.1097/00004583-199303000-00010

Serbin, L., Poulin-Dubois, D., Colburne, K. A., Sen, M. G., & Eichstedt, J. A (2001). Gender stereotyping in infancy: Visual preferences for and knowledge of gender-stereotyped toys in the second year. *The International Society for the Study of Behavioral Development, 25*(1), 7–15. https://doi.org/10.1080/00221325.1985.9923457

Shields, J. P., Cohen, R., Glassman, J. R., Whitaker, K., Franks, H., & Bertolini, I. (2013). Estimating population size and demographic characteristics of lesbian, gay, bisexual, and transgender youth in middle school. *Journal of Adolescent Health, 52*(2), 248–250.

Shutts, K., Kenward, B., Falk, H., Ivegran, A., & Fawcett, C. (2017). Early preschool environments and gender: Effects of gender pedagogy in Sweden. *Journal of Experimental Child Psychology, 162*, 1–17.

Shutts, K., Roben, C. K. P., & Spelke, E. S. (2013). Children's use of social categories in thinking about people and social relationships. *Journal of Cognition and Development, 14*(1), 35–62.

Signorella, M. L., Bigler, R. S., & Liben, L. S. (1993). Developmental differences in children's gender schemata about others: A metaanalytic review. *Developmental Review, 13*(2), 147–183. https://doi.org/10.1006/drev.1993.1007

Silva, J. M., Langhout, R. D., Kohfeldt, D., & Gurrola, E. (2015). "Good" and "bad" kids? A race and gender analysis of effective behavioral support in an elementary school. *Urban Education, 50*(7), 787–811.

Simpkins, S. D., Price, C. D., & Garcia, K. (2015). Parental support and high school students' motivation in biology, chemistry, and physics: Understanding differences among Latino and Caucasian boys and girls. *Journal of Research in Science Teaching, 52*(10), 1386–1407. https://doi.org/10.1002/tea.21246

Skeat, J., Wake, M., Reilly, S. et al. (2010). Predictors of early precocious talking: A prospective population study. *Journal of Child Language, 37*(5), 1109–1121. https://doi.org/10.1017/S030500090999016X

Skiba, R. J., Michael, R. S., Nardo, A. C., & Peterson, R. L. (2002). The color of discipline: Sources of racial and gender disproportionality in school punishment. *The Urban Review, 34*(4), 317–342. https://doi.org/10.1023/A:1021320817372

Swedish National Agency for Education. (2011). *Curriculum for the compulsory school, preschool class and the recreation centre.*

Slaby, R. G., & Frey, K. S. (1975). Development of gender constancy and selective attention to same-sex models. *Child Development, 46*(4), 849–856. https://doi.org/10.2307/1128389

Slater, A., & Tiggemann, M. (2016). Little girls in a grown up world: Exposure to sexualized media, internalization of sexualization messages, and body image in 6–9 year-old girls. *Body Image, 18*, 19–22.

Starr, C. R., & Zurbriggen, E. L. (2019). Self-sexualization in preadolescent girls: Associations with self-objectification, weight concerns, and parent's academic expectations. *International Journal of Behavioral Development, 43*(6), 515–522.

Steffens, M. C., & Jelenec, P. (2011). Separating implicit gender stereotypes regarding math and language: Implicit ability stereotypes are self-serving for boys and men, but not for girls and women. *Sex Roles, 64*(5–6), 324–335.

Steffens, M. C., Jelenec, P., & Noack, P. (2010). On the leaky math pipeline: Comparing implicit math-gender stereotypes and math withdrawal in female and male children and adolescents. *Journal of Educational Psychology, 102*(4), 947–963.

Stennes, L. M., Burch, M. M., Sen, M. G., & Bauer, P. J. (2005). A longitudinal study of gendered vocabulary and communicative action in young children. *Developmental Psychology, 41*(1), 75–88. https://doi.org/10.1037/0012-1649.41.1.75

Stewart, S. M., Bond, M. H., Abdullah, A. M., & Ma, S. L. (2000). Gender, parenting, and adolescent functioning in Bangladesh. *Merrill-Palmer Quarterly, 46*(3),540–564.

Stewart, S. M., Bond, M. H., Ho, L. M., Zaman, R. M., Dar, R., & Anwar, M. (2000). Perceptions of parents and adolescent outcomes in Pakistan. *British Journal of Developmental Psychology, 18*(3),335–352. https://doi.org/10 .1348/026151000165733

Stone, E. A., Brown, C. S., & Jewell, J. A. (2015). The sexualized girl: A within-gender stereotype among elementary school children. *Child Development, 86*(5), 1604–1622.

Strough, J., & Covatto, A. M. (2002). Context and age differences in same-and other-gender peer preferences. *Social Development, 11*(3), 346–361.

Suárez-Orozco, C., & Qin, D. B. (2006). Gendered perspectives in psychology: Immigrant origin youth. *International Migration Review, 40*(1), 165–198.

Tate, C. C., Ledbetter, J. N., & Youssef, C. P. (2013). A two-question method for assessing gender categories in the social and medical sciences. *Journal of Sex Research, 50*(8), 767–776.

Temkin, D., Belford, J., McDaniel, T., Stratford, B., & Parris, D. (2017). *Improving measurement of sexual orientation and gender identity among middle and high school students.* Bethesda, MD: Child Trends.

Tenenbaum, H. R., & Leaper, C. (2003). Parent-child conversations about science: The socialization of gender inequities?. *Developmental Psychology, 39*(1), 34–47. https://doi.org/10.1037/0012-1649.39.1.34

Tiggemann, M., & Slater, A. (2014). NetTweens: The internet and body image concerns in preteenage girls. *The Journal of Early Adolescence, 34*(5), 606–620.

Tomasello, M. (2019). *Becoming human: A theory of ontogeny.* Cambridge, MA: Belknap Press.

Tomasello, M., Mannle, S., & Kruger, A. C. (1986). Linguistic environment of 1-to 2-year-old twins. *Developmental Psychology, 22*(2), 169.

Trautner, H. M., Ruble, D. N., Cyphers, L., Kirsten, B., Behrendt, R., & Hartmann, P. (2005). Rigidity and flexibility of gender stereotypes in child-hood: Developmental or differential?. *Infant and Child Development: An International Journal of Research and Practice, 14*(4), 365–381.

UNESCO (United Nations Educational, Scientific, and Cultural Organization). (2010). *World atlas of gender equity in education.* Paris: UNESCO.

UNESCO (United Nations Educational, Scientific, and Cultural Organization). (2016). *Creating sustainable futures for all.* Global education monitoring report: gender review. https://unesdoc.unesco.org/ark:/48223/pf0000246045

Valenzuela, A., Jr. (1999). Gender roles and settlement activities among children and their immigrant families. *American Behavioral Scientist, 42*(4), 720–742.

Valenzuela, A., & Dornbusch, S. M. (1994). Familism and social capital in the academic achievement of Mexican origin and Anglo adolescents. *Social Science Quarterly, 75*(1), 18–36.

van Anders, S. M. (2015). Beyond sexual orientation: Integrating gender/sex and diverse sexualities via sexual configurations theory. *Archives of Sexual Behavior, 44*(5), 1177–1213.

van Anders, S. M., Goldey, K. L., & Bell, S. N. (2014). Measurement of testosterone in human sexuality research: Methodological considerations. *Archives of Sexual Behavior, 43*(2), 231–250. https://doi.org/10 .1007/s10508-013-0123-z

van de Beek, C., van Goozen, S. H., Buitelaar, J. K., & Cohen-Kettenis, P. T. (2009). Prenatal sex hormones (maternal and amniotic fluid) and gender-related play behavior in 13-month-old infants. *Archives of Sexual Behavior, 38*(1), 6–15.

Vandermaas-Peeler, M., Sassine, B., Price, C., & Brilhart, C. (2012). Mothers' and fathers' guidance behaviours during storybook reading. *Journal of Early Childhood Literacy, 12*(4), 415–442.

van der Pol, L. D., Groeneveld, M. G., van Berkel, S. R. et al. (2015). Fathers' and mothers' emotion talk with their girls and boys from toddlerhood to preschool age. *Emotion, 15*(6), 854.

Vasey, P. L., & Bartlett, N. H. (2007). What can the Samoan "Fa'afafine" teach us about the Western concept of gender identity disorder in childhood?. *Perspectives in Biology and Medicine, 50*(4), 481–490.

Vekiri, I., & Chronaki, A. (2008). Gender issues in technology use: Perceived social support, computer self-efficacy and value beliefs, and computer use beyond school. *Computers & Education, 51*(3), 1392–1404.

Wallace, J. M., Goodkind, S., Wallace, C. M., & Bachman, J. G. (2008). Racial, ethnic, and gender differences in school discipline among U.S. high school students: 1991–2005. *The Negro Educational Review, 59*(1–2), 47–62.

Weisgram, E. S., & Dinella, L. M. (2018). *Gender typing of children's toys: How early play experiences impact development.* Washington, DC: American Psychological Association.

Whitehouse, A. O. (2010). Is there a sex ratio difference in the familial aggregation of specific language impairment? A meta-analysis. *Journal of Speech, Language, and Hearing Research, 53*(4), 1015–1025. https://doi.org /10.1044/1092-4388(2009/09-0078)

WHO (World Health Organization). (2018). *Gender, health and the 2030 agenda for sustainable development.* www.who.int/bulletin/volumes/96/9/ 18-211607.pdf

Wood, E., Desmarais, S., & Gugula, S. (2002). The impact of parenting experience on gender stereotyped toy play of children. *Sex Roles, 47*(1–2), 39–49.

Wood, W., & Eagly, A. H. (2002). A cross-cultural analysis of the behavior of women and men: Implications for the origins of sex differences. *Psychological bulletin, 128*(5), 699–727. https://doi.org/10.1037/0033-2909 .128.5.699

Xiao, S. X., Cook, R. E., Martin, C. L., & Nielson, M. G. (2019). Characteristics of preschool gender enforcers and peers who associate with them. *Sex Roles, 81*(11–12), 671–685.

Yee, D. K., & Eccles, J. S. (1988). Parent perceptions and attributions for children's math achievement. *Sex Roles, 19*(5–6), 317–333. https://doi.org /10.1007/BF00289840

Yeung, S. P., & Wong, W. I. (2018). Gender labels on gender-neutral colors: Do they affect children's color preferences and play performance?. *Sex Roles, 79*(5–6), 260–272.

Young, R., & Sweeting, H. (2004). Adolescent bullying, relationships, psychological well-being, and gender-atypical behavior: A gender diagnosticity approach. *Sex Roles, 50*(7–8), 525–537.

Zambrana, I. M., Ystrom, E., & Pons, F. (2012). Impact of gender, maternal education, and birth order on the development of language comprehension: A longitudinal study from 18 to 36 months of age. *Journal of Developmental & Behavioral Pediatrics, 33*(2), 146–155. https://doi.org/10.1097/DBP .0b013e31823d4f83

Zosuls, K. M., Andrews, N. C., Martin, C. L., England, D. E., & Field, R. D. (2016). Developmental changes in the link between gender typicality and peer victimization and exclusion. *Sex Roles, 75*(5–6), 243–256.

Zosuls, K. M., Miller, C. F., Ruble, D. N., Martin, C. L., & Fabes, R. A. (2011). Gender development research in sex roles: Historical trends and future directions. *Sex Roles, 64*(11–12), 826–842.

Zosuls, K. M., Ruble, D. N., Tamis-LeMonda, C. S., Shrout, P. E., Bornstein, M. H., & Greulich, F. K. (2009). The acquisition of gender labels in infancy: Implications for gender-typed play. *Developmental Psychology, 45*(3), 688–701. https://doi.org/10.1037/a0014053

Cambridge Elements ≡

Child Development

Marc H. Bornstein
National Institute of Child Health and Human Development, Bethesda
Institute for Fiscal Studies, London
UNICEF, New York City
Marc H. Bornstein is an Affiliate of the *Eunice Kennedy Shriver* National Institute of Child
Health and Human Development, an International Research Fellow at the Institute for Fiscal
Studies (London), and UNICEF Senior Advisor for Research for ECD Parenting Programmes.
Bornstein is President Emeritus of the Society for Research in Child Development,
Editor Emeritus of *Child Development*, and founding Editor of *Parenting: Science and
Practice*.

About the Series
Child development is a lively and engaging, yet serious and purposeful subject of academic
study that encompasses myriad of theories, methods, substantive areas, and applied
concerns. Cambridge Elements in Child Development proposes to address all these key
areas, with unique, comprehensive, and state-of-the-art treatments, introducing readers
to the primary currents of research and to original perspectives on, or contributions to,
principal issues and domains in the field.

Cambridge Elements $\equiv$

Child Development

Elements in the Series

Child Development in Evolutionary Perspective
David F. Bjorklund

Gender in Childhood
Christia Spears Brown, Sharla D. Biefeld and Michelle J. Tam

A full series listing is available at: www.cambridge.org/EICD

Printed in the United States
By Bookmasters